TRANSFER PRINTING
onto man-made fibres

Overleaf Designs from the Sublistatic Library, Geneva

TRANSFER PRINTING
onto man-made fibres

GUY SCOTT

CHARLES T. BRANFORD CO. NEWTON CENTRE, MASS.

First published 1977
US ISBN 1-8231-7036-5
Printed in Great Britain

Chas. T. Branford Co
Newton Centre, Mass. 02159

Contents

Acknowledgment

First I would like to thank Brian Eastwood ATI, Senior Lecturer in Textiles at Leicester Polytechnic, for his great assistance in the preparation of this book and also for supplying so much practical information on the technique of transfer printing. Similarly I would like to thank Ken Consterdine, Development Manager of Bemrose Corporation, Derby, for allowing me to use his own technical lecture notes as reference material for this work. Without the assistance of both gentlemen this book would not have been possible.

My sincere appreciation goes to Geraldine Knowles, John Beedle, Binney Hale and Christopher Hawkins for supplying so many of the photographs, and to Transprints (UK) Limited, producers of photogravure transfer printing papers, for colour plates facing pages 96 and 97.

My thanks to all the children, students, teachers and designers whose work appears in this book, and in particular Jane Gabrielle Scott, Rita Davis, Peter Barker, Frank Birtwhistle and the Studio of Binney and Smith Inc, New York. I would also like to thank Joan Aldridge, Head of Printed Textiles, Leicester Polytechnic, for allowing me to use examples of her students' work and take photographs of her department.

My sincere thanks to Barbara Aitken for correcting and typing the various drafts of this book so carefully and to Thelma M Nye, my editor, who patiently encouraged me to finish the book, many months after the completion date.

Finally I would like to thank all the people and firms concerned in commercial transfer printing who have given me invaluable assistance by supplying technical information and photographs, and these are listed at the back of the book.

Guy Scott
Dadford 1976

Foreword

The traditional methods of creating designs onto fabric can broadly be summarized as tie-dye, batik, block printing, screen printing, stencils and free brush work. All these processes have been successfully adapted for school use with children of all ages. What has always been lacking was a simple print process which allowed the students to work on paper and then accurately translate their designs onto fabric, without the need of sophisticated techniques or equipment. In the same field the majority of these traditional methods were developed solely for cotton, and the dyes available were not suitable for the vast range of synthetic fabrics which have come on to the market in the past two decades; bearing both these considerations in mind one can see the significance and design potential of transfer printing.

Introduction

Although transfer printing is a relatively new textile printing technique many examples of this process can be seen in nearly every department store and boutique. Many colleges and schools are beginning to realise the potential of this print process in terms of design education.

The term 'transfer' printing is possibly misleading, as one immediately thinks of the transfers which are particularly popular on cotton tee shirts. This is not true transfer printing, but a hot melt process which allows the design to be stuck onto the surface of the fabric, in a rather harsh plastic coating.

The subject of this book is the history, technology, design potential and future development of the vapour diffusion and solid state dyeing process called *transfer printing* or 'sublistatic printing'.

A factor which must be stressed at the start is that transfer printing is suitable for use mainly on man-made fibres. Although one might feel that this is a disadvantage, more and more synthetic fabrics are being used. Consequently the resulting knowledge, which comes from the study of these synthetic fabrics, is bound to be of value to the textile designer.

At the present time there is no similar system available for printing natural fibres, although recent research has produced a method of working which allows the base material, ie cotton or rayon, to be impregnated with a synthetic medium and so allow it to be successfully transfer-printed. However, this process is still at the research stage and consequently is only dealt with briefly. But as the design technique and indeed the transfer process are exactly the same as for synthetic fibres, the information given throughout the book will still be relevant when this most recent research does ultimately enlarge the scope of transfer printing in schools and colleges. Likewise at the commercial level a number of systems have already been patented and, in fact, a process for wool is already a commercial proposition. In chapter 10 details are given of the various research projects into the feasibility of transfer printing onto natural materials, and the possibilities of printing, by this technique, surfaces such as acrylic sheet and aluminium.

I will start by looking briefly at the history of transfer printing, which is a fascinating story of modern technological research, and I will then try and show how the implications of this commercial process can be logically related to the needs of the art teacher. At this stage I would like to emphasize that although some areas of the book are technical, so that students can develop their work to professional standards, the technique of transfer printing, by definition, is so simple that many of the design processes discussed can easily be applied to the primary school, as we can see illustrated in chapter 4.

1 The history of transfer printing

Transfer prints on textiles have been produced in a variety of forms for at least a century. The earliest form being an embroidery transfer applied by a hot iron to the background material which was usually linen or cotton. The design was then decorated with stitches. These early designs were produced from printing inks, containing shellac and coloured pigment, usually ultramarine.

The concept of transfer printing dates back almost to the first commercial introduction of disperse dyes in 1924 and was mentioned in two British patents in 1929 and 1931. In 1958 Noel De Plasse, Chief Chemical Engineer to the French textile company Prouvost-Masurel, demonstrated the principle of printing paper with dyes which were capable of sublimation; that is they could be vaporized and transferred to a synthetic fabric by the application of heat on to the back of the paper design.

A number of years were required to develop the process to a commercial and practical stage, but one had in these early experiments the beginnings of a textile process which has revolutionized the printing of synthetic fabrics in industry, and in turn has the potential of creating a range of educational products, such as transfer crayons and transfer inks, which could radically change the teaching of textiles in schools and colleges over the next few years. This process gives the designer the freedom to directly transfer his paper design permanently and accurately onto a wide range of fabrics, simply by the application of heat; from an ordinary domestic iron or a purpose built transfer press.

The background to transfer printing

The most interesting feature of transfer printing is that it relies upon the phenomenon of 'vapour diffusion' which hitherto had been considered in the textile trade as a failing of certain dyestuffs belonging to the dispersed dye class. During the industrial processing of prints, or dyeing of fabrics constructed from man-made fibres, the penultimate stage is a vigorous washing action. This is followed by drying the fabric in a continuous manner by passing it through heated chambers at a high temperature. It was during this process that it was noticed, on occasions, that some fabrics would emerge with specks of colour deposited haphazardly upon them. This was due to a property possessed by certain chemicals, including some members of the dispersed dye class, termed *sublimation*.

Sublimation is a term given when one heats a solid compound which then passes directly to a gaseous form but reverts to a solid state again upon touching a cool surface. Because of this chemical action, dyestuffs from the fabric, being dried at high temperatures, could vaporize allowing the gaseous particles to float in the drying chamber. These would then be reconverted into solid particles in the cooler parts of the drying chamber and drop back on to the fabric as solid specks of colour.

In the early 1950s this inherent failing was recognised as providing the basis for a unique method of printing and the first patent was taken out in 1960. As mentioned earlier this initial development was carried out by a European consortium and, although many problems had to be resolved concerning the availability of suitable papers and transfer presses, the first commercial transfer paper, bearing the appropriate trade name of *Sublistatic*, came on the market in 1968. This created an enormous amount of interest within the industry and several leading European and American companies, specialising in textile printing, ink manufacture and paper printing, began to develop similar products in the early 1970s.

The process of transfer printing has had an enthusiastic reception from fabric and garment producers throughout the world.

The commercial application

To appreciate the full implications of transfer printing it is important to ask why this process exists and what are the reasons for its growth and obvious potential. Without going into the economic considerations too deeply the main advantages can be summarized as follows:

1 As one is initially printing the design on to a paper substrate one can see that paper is a much better surface on which to print as it is dimensionally stable, and smooth. Unlike fabric it does not stretch or wrinkle, or have a fuzzy texture. The printing of some synthetic materials often created problems when using traditional methods, therefore one is able to produce perfect registration of a complicated design, in a number of colours, as all colours are printed at one time. For the same reason the texture or pile of the fabric is not critical and designs can be applied to either the lightest fabric or a heavy piled carpet with equal success.

2 Since all the technical work has been carried out by the printers of the papers, the knitting industry (where this process is particularly popular) can easily and quickly train operatives to carry out the transferring

Engraved cylinders in Sublistatic's factory in Taucering, France

Printing fully fashioned garments from transfer paper, Sublistatic factory on a Kaunegressee press

Machine used to test new engraved cylinders and new colour combinations. Sublistatic factory Isabella, Puerto Rico

operation. It has become an ideal method of printing fully fashioned sweaters, or sections of garments, which are afterwards made up on the 'cut and sew' principle.

3 For the reasons outlined above the manufacturer can now print garments front and back with relatively unskilled labour and with the minimum of spoilt work. As the time of operation can be only 2 to 3 minutes for each garment, this allows the knitting manufacturer to limit his work to making plain white or dyed garments and then to print these as his customers require them. One can easily appreciate the danger of commissioning thousands of metres/yards of a printed fabric from an orthodox printer, making up into garments, and then finding that some designs or colour-ways will not sell. In the same area one sees the garment makers and knitters being able to produce their own range of designs and so create a complete end product instead of only the half product.

The process is still firmly based upon sublimation, but additionally and simultaneously involves a technique called *solid state dyeing*. This means that the paper is printed (in a traditional method ie gravure, flexographic, rotary screen etc, (see summary of these processes in chapter 8) with dyestuffs of the dispersed class, which will vaporize upon heating. After the printed paper is dried it is then placed in contact with a fabric made from man-made fibres (see fabric selection) and heated in a press for say 20 seconds at 205°C. The dyes will then vaporize but have no opportunity to condense as solid particles. Instead the vapour diffuses into the fibres and dissolves in them. The sandwich of paper and fabric is then separated after the pressing operation to show a dramatic change in colour. The dye remaining upon the paper is dull and uninteresting whilst the colour upon the fabric is bright and strong. This is because it is only when the dyes dissolve in the fibres that the true colours are revealed.

Although there are many dyes from the dispersed class which vaporize, practical considerations of maximum colour yield, fastness to light and washing, restricts the number used to about twelve different dyestuffs. However, these can be used in mixtures with each other to give a wide range of shades.

Once the pressing operation has been carried out no further work is required since the dyes are now fully fixed upon the fabric. With the present concern into the problems of pollution it is significant to note that transfer printing uses no water and yields no effluent for disposal, unlike the traditional methods of dyeing and finishing fabric.*

*In 1976, 7·6 per cent of all capital investment in the textile field, within the USA was for pollution control.

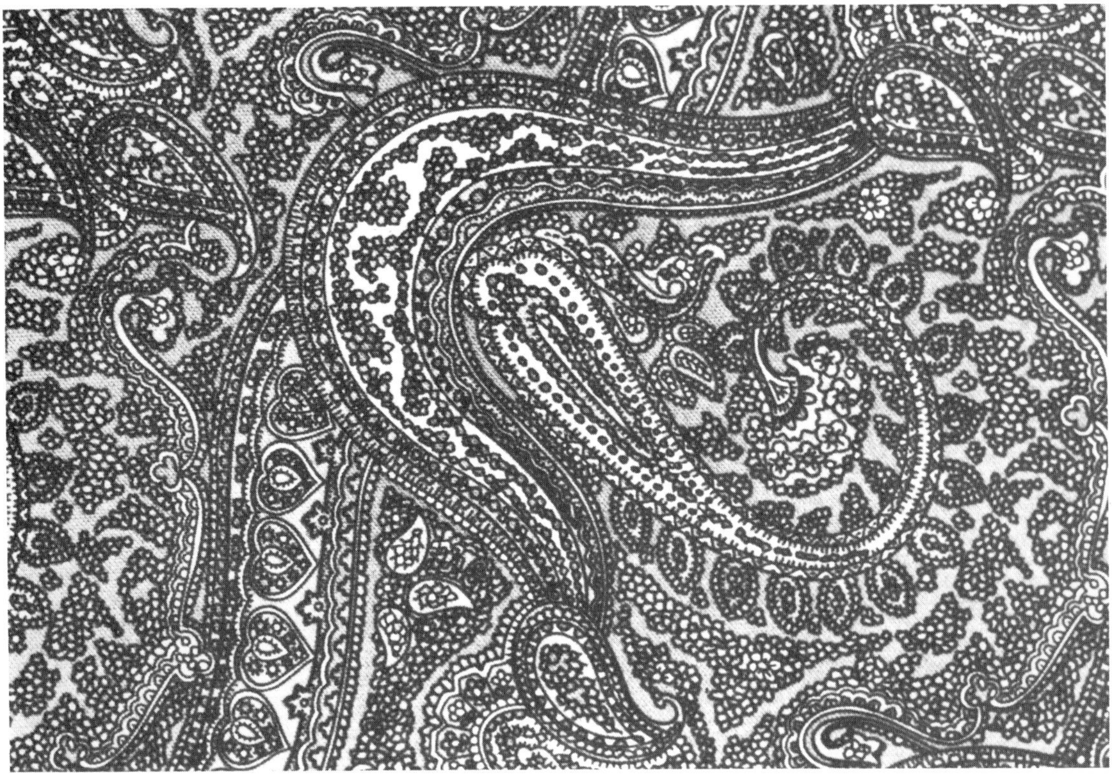

Detail of a Paisley design which has been transfer printed with a paper produced on a Flexotex 1900, 74 in. (1·8 m) wide common impression flexographic printing press (Strachan Henslaw)

Two detailed transfer prints in contrasting styles. Designs by Sublistatic Geneva

2 Choice of fabrics

As is generally accepted, the area of the textile market, which was previously the stronghold of natural and animal fibres such as cotton and wool, has now become dominated by man-made fibres mainly due to cost and availability. However the advent of these fibres has presented the teacher with many problems, as the majority of textile colours were developed solely for cotton, and as these new fibres tend to be relatively non-absorbent to water, they are difficult to colour permanently unless sophisticated equipment is used.

With the introduction of first transfer crayons, and more recently the use of transfer inks, the printing of synthetic fabrics has become much more viable in schools and colleges and exciting work can be achieved.

Unfortunately our knowledge of man-made fibres tends to be superficial and as most of our purchases are made either on the local market or in chain stores (with unskilled assistants) it is exceptionally difficult to obtain exact information on the particular type of synthetic fabric which has been purchased.

For this reason a section on fabric definition related to their suitability for transfer printing might be of particular relevance at this stage.

To return to my original comments concerning the difficulties encountered when printing man-made fabrics with traditional inks, these difficulties can be related to the various types of synthetics as follows, with number 1 as the most difficult:

1 Polyester. 2 Acrylic. 3 Triacetate. 4 Polyamides. 5 Diacetate.

The process of transfer printing has the remarkable inherent advantages of reversing this sequence, so that the polyester fibres become the easiest to colour. Since certain fibres (such as rayon) will not accept transfer colours it is obviously very important to be able to identify easily a fibre which will transfer permanently.

The following form of identification is given only as a simple method of identification, for, as can be appreciated, precise fibre identification is a highly skilled technology. However, this process has been used successfully for ten years in a college, with relatively unskilled first year students, for the only requirements of the person operating the tests are careful observation and a good sense of smell. The equipment required is also simple, as all one needs is a box of matches and a bottle of *Acetone* (or nail varnish remover). The obvious inflammable nature of both these materials should, of course, be carefully noted.

Test showing the type of effects obtained when various synthetic fabrics are exposed to heat

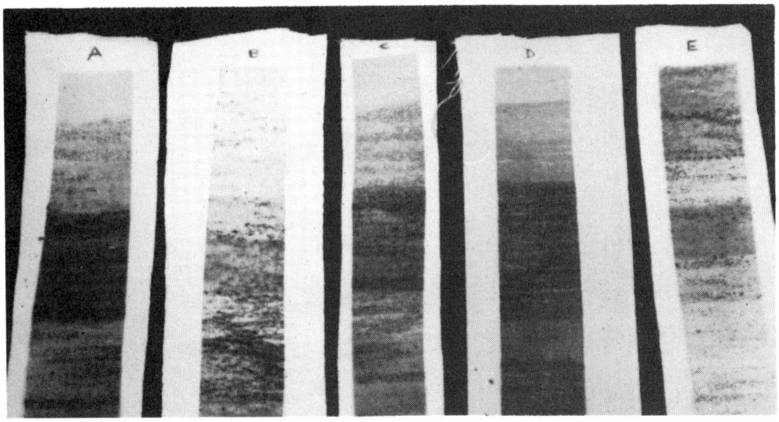

Simple test showing the difference obtained in terms of colour fastness, when different types of fabric are transfer printed. Reference: **A** Nylon, **B** Wool, **C** Terylene/Cotton, **D** Crimplene, **E** Cotton

For safety reasons this type of basic fibre research could quite easily be carried out in conjunction with the science department, and indeed a more analytical approach will usually produce the most valuable results. In the same way projects dealing with 'colour fastness' and 'light fastness' would also be interesting assignments for the home economics department, as well as for the design student.

Listed below are the various tests recommended to assess fibre suitability for transfer printing.

Test 1

Take a small bunch of fibres, or small piece of fabric and ignite it.

(a) Examine the flame carefully, particularly the area of the tip and 50–76 mm (2–3 in.) above.

(b) Extinguish the flame and carefully smell it.

(c) Examine the burnt residue.

The following specific reactions take place with appropriate groups of fibres enabling conclusions to be made.

*The most important characteristic is specially indicated.

Group 1

(a) Burns readily.

(b) Strong smell of burning paper.*

(c) A black crushable residue.

Conclusion: Cellulosic fibres eg Cotton, Flex jute. Regenerated cellulosic rayons eg Viscose, Evlan, Sarille.

NOT SUITABLE FOR TRANSFER PRINTING

Group II

(a) Burns with a spluttering flame.
(b) Strong smell of burning hair or feathers.*
(c) A soft black residue.

Conclusion: Animal fibres eg wool or silk.
NOT SUITABLE FOR TRANSFER PRINTING

Group III

(a) Does not burn easily.
(b) Strong smell of burning celery.*
(c) A hard fawn coloured bead residue.*

Caution: During the burning test molten drops will fall from the test sample. If these fall on the skin they stick and could give a painful burn.
Conclusion: Polyamide eg Nylon, Perlon.
SUITABLE FOR TRANSFER PRINTING.

Group IV

(a) Burns easily, flame shows pronounced smokey cap like a candle flame or badly trimmed oil lamp.*
(b) Strong smell difficult to identify or remember.
(c) A black hard residue.

Conclusion: Acrylic eg Orlon, Courtelle, Acrilon.
SUITABLE FOR TRANSFER PRINTING.

Test 2

Take a small piece of fibre or fabric and place in a suitable container. Cover with acetone* or nail varnish remover.

Group V

The material dissolves *completely* in one minute or less.
Conclusion: Diacetate eg Dicel.
SUITABLE FOR TRANSFER PRINTING.

Group VI

The material partly dissolves to form a gelatinous mass, in 1 minute or less.
Conclusion: Triacetate eg Tricel.
SUITABLE FOR TRANSFER PRINTING.

Group VII

Tests numbers 1 and 2 are designed to give an immediate response from the observer. The members of this group are obtained by achieving negative answers to the tests. Therefore a fibre which fails to clearly identify itself by burning or dissolving is in all probability a member of the family called Polyesters eg Terylene, Dacron, Trevira.
SUITABLE FOR TRANSFER PRINTING.
It should be noted that a fibre which refuses to burn will be glass fibre or asbestos and therefore unsuitable for transfer printing.

*Acetone gives the most reliable results for this type of work and is usually obtained from chemists. When carrying out the tests ensure first of all that the container will withstand the solvent action, ie do not store in a plastic bottle.

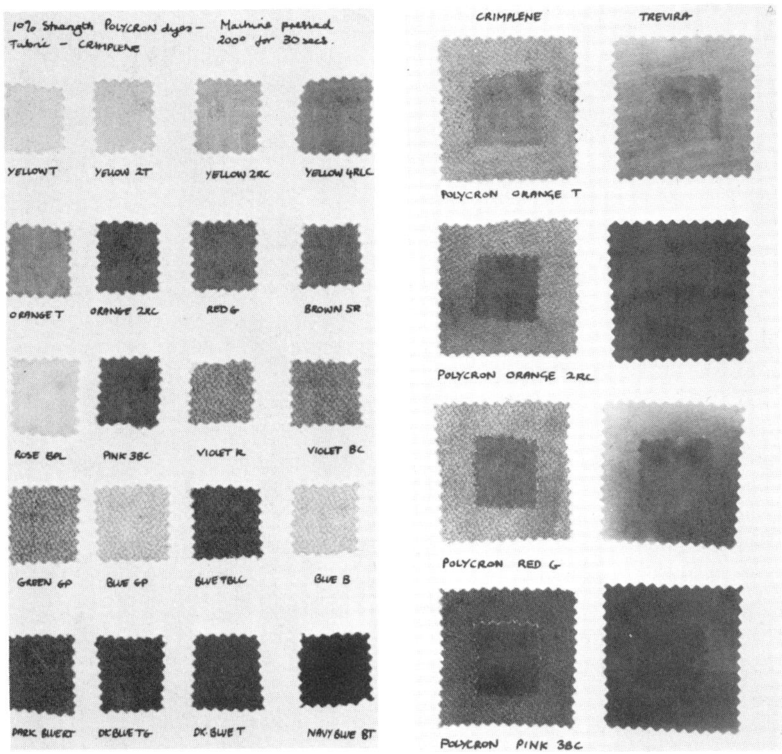

The assessment of different disperse colours. Even at this stage the student is able to deduce which colour range is most suitable for his particular requirements

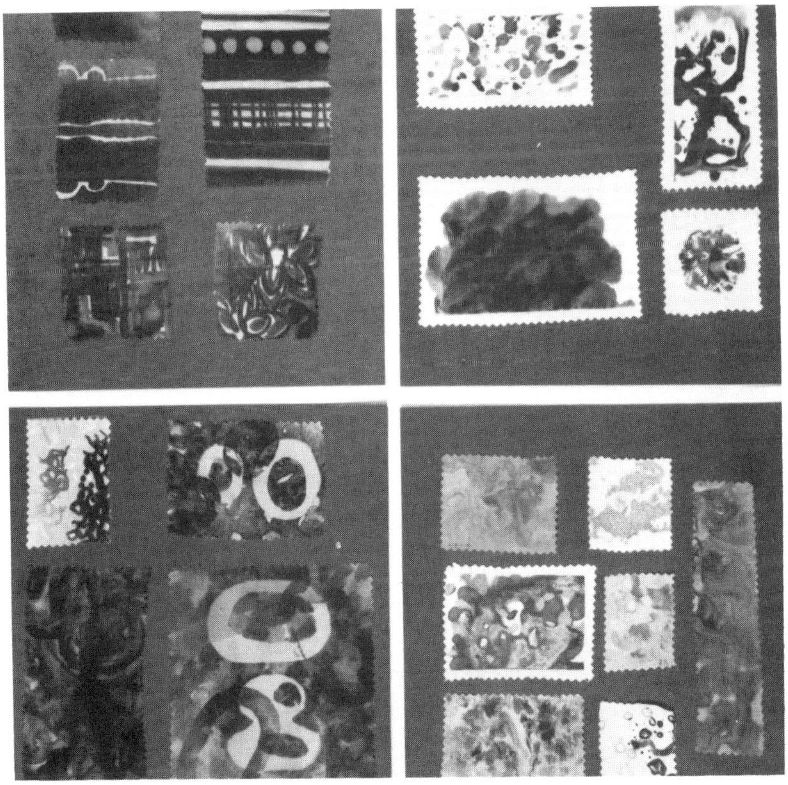

Four sheets of experiments using transfer crayons and transfer inks. Sheet 1 shows the different effect achieved when the temperature of the iron or press is varied. Sheet 2 illustrates the variety of textures which can be achieved when algenate and water are added to the aqueous transfer dyes. Sheet 3 explores the technique of overprinting and masking areas of the design surface. Sheet 4 uses similar techniques to sheet 2, but prints the final papers onto a variety of different fabrics from thin nylon net to very thick crimplene

Mixtures

The fibres in groups III to VII are suitable for transfer printing even when mixed with fibres from groups I and II to produce blended fabrics. The mixing of fibres by manufacturers is a well established practice, so it is common to have a fabric of say Terylene/cotton, thus having one transferrable component and one non-transferrable component. Such blended fabrics should not be considered unsuitable for transfer printing as much depends upon the relative proportions of the fibres. For example, the intensity of colour given on a Terylene/cotton fabric will undoubtedly be less than on a 100% Terylene fabric, but the degree of intensity will, of course, depend upon the extent of the dilution of the total fibre content by the cotton. So one should aim to use blended fabrics where the percentage content of the transferrable material is as high as possible. This conclusion sounds rather complex but as test samples can be printed so easily, the designer can soon decide if a given fabric is suitable for his needs and when engaged in this experimental stage some fascinating and unexpected results can be achieved, both using the transfer crayons and transfer inks.

To conclude this type of research, one can see how some students might be motivated to look at fabrics and their construction in some depth. The following brief summary of synthetic fabric terms, taken from two excellent wall charts published by British Sewing Ltd called *Natural Fibres and Man-Made Fibres*, could easily be used to establish this work as a study of materials which are constantly encountered by the student every day of his life.

Summary of man-made fibres

Synthetic fabrics can be divided into three sections:

1 Products made from cellulose in wood pulp and cotton linters. First made in the eighteenth century and developed as viscose rayon cellulose acetate and cellulose triacetate.

2 Products from liquids and gases in petroleum and coal. First made in 1939 and developed into polyamides, polyesters, acrylics, polypropylene and elastanes.

3 Made from minerals for special purposes such as glass fibre, asbestos and aluminium.

As has been emphasised Group I is not readily suitable for transfer printing. Group II is most suitable for this print process and group III is not immediately acceptable for transfer printing methods. However as we will see later in the book a material such as aluminium can be treated to allow the surface to accept the transfer dyes.

In addition it is important to remember that within these broad groupings fabrics vary enormously because of the weight and type of yarn used, the method of weaving or knitting, the dyeing and printing of the fabric and finally the finish which can be applied to the fabric to give it particular characteristics, ie water resistant finishes for raincoats, long lasting creases for trousers, etc.

As we are particularly concerned with Group II in terms of transfer printing, I have listed below their chemical categories, related them to the household names which are more familiar, and then outlined briefly their source of production and main characteristics.

Acrylics

Trade names: *Orlon*, *Acrilan*, *Courtelle* and *Dralon*.

The first acrylic fibre came on the market in 1950 and all acrylic fibres are made of, at least, 85% acrylonitrile, a liquid produced in oil refining and coal carbonisation. Acrylic fabrics are soft and warm to the touch and are often used as a substitute for wool. They are crease resistant, do not shrink or felt, and wear particularly well.

They are used mainly for: sweaters, jersey fabrics, babywear, brushed fabrics, deep pile fabrics and woven flannel. In the home they can be used for: curtains, blankets, carpets, upholstery fabrics and paint rollers.

Polyesters

Trade names: *Dacron*, *Terylene*, *Crimplene*, *Terlenka*, *Trevira*, *Diolen* and *Linelle*.

First manufactured in the United States as Dacron in 1953, polyesters are melt-spun like nylon but use teraphthalic acid derived from petroleum. Polyester fabrics wear particularly well, do not shrink and are crease resistant. When blended with wool or cotton, polyesters give the same care characteristics as these fibres and can be permanently heat-set into pleats etc. very satisfactorily. If made into a soft fluffy wadding they can be used as a filling.

Uses: Fashion – blouses, dresses, and as crimplene for knitted outerwear, as *Fiberfill* it is used in anoraks, and housecoats and as a wool or cotton blend in men's and women's outerwear. In the home one sees these fibres used for bedlinen (blended with cotton), carpets, and as *Fiberfill* in duvets, pillows, sleeping bags and upholstered furniture.

Dressmaking note: If these fabrics are to be used in home dressmaking, a synthetic sewing thread should be used, such as *Trylko*.

Polyamides

(Nylon: developed simultaneously in New York and London, hence the name). Trade names: *Antron, Bri-nylon, Cantrece, Cellon, Enkalon, Qiana*.

The process of making nylon was discovered in 1938 and has since developed into more than 1000 types. All nylons are made from chemicals present in petroleum and coal which are melted and then spun to produce filaments of long molecules called polyamides. As one would expect the properties of nylon fabrics depend on the weight, weave and finish of the particular type. Generally nylon does not absorb moisture and soils easily, but it does clean very easily, will not shrink and is very hard wearing. It does tend to yellow but new processes recently introduced have helped to overcome this problem.

Uses: Fashion – hosiery, underwear, men's socks, children's wear, overalls, knitwear, swimwear, foundation garments and rainwear. Also blended with wool for warmth and made into luxury silk-like fabrics for ties and dresses, etc. Household – sheets, curtains, upholstery, carpets and stretched covers.

Polyurethanes

Trade names: *Lycra*, *Spanzelle*.

The fibres in this group are more elastic than rubber and yet are stronger and lighter.

Uses: Fashion – foundation garments, support hose, swimwear.

Polyurethane finishes are also used in the coating of other materials such as leather to allow the base material to accept transfer printing. This process is also being used to transfer print cotton fabric, but here the polyurethane is incorporated into the transfer paper.

Polypropylene

Trade names: *Courlene, Typor, Ulstron, Meraklon.*

Polypropylene is a recently developed man-made fibre with enormous potential. It was developed by the scientists who won the 1963 Nobel Prize for Chemistry. In this process petroleum gas is converted chemically into tiny pellets which are then melted and spun into very light and strong fibres which are relatively inexpensive.

Uses: Fashion – socks, sweaters, one-way nappies (and knitted fabrics which are totally water resistant). Household – blankets, carpets, carpet backing, upholstery and outdoor carpets for artificial lawns and sport surfaces.

The complete 'Learning about Sewing' package produced by English Sewing Ltd. The two wall charts are of particular interest, as one deals with man-made fibres and the other with material fabrics. Project sheets and examples are also included

3 Transfer printing using transfer crayons

Transfer colours can be applied in the form of ink or as transfer crayons, and as this latter form is more applicable to younger children and for all students to make their initial transfer experiments, I will deal with this dry method of transfer printing first.

Transfer crayons have been on the market for the past five years and were originally developed by Binney and Smith, in conjunction with Brian Eastwood a textile consultant. They are available in eight different colours and look like conventional wax crayons. This is however where the similarity ends. By using the most recent dye technology the manufacturers have been able to suspend the transfer colours in a wax binder, thus creating a range of colours that can easily be used on paper and then transferred onto synthetic fabrics by ironing with an ordinary domestic iron, or by the use of a transfer press (see page 121).

Colour mixing

Although only eight colours are available a great variety of other colours and tones can be achieved simply by overlaying the different colours directly on the paper before transfer. Another method, which is possibly more successful, is to transfer differently coloured papers one after another onto the fabric. This technique not only gives a greater intensity of colour from the subsequent mixtures, but also allows textured rubbings to be included.

Experimental stage (see list of suitable fabrics and method of working pages 14 and 21)

Transfer crayons write and handle like conventional wax crayons but after transfer from paper to fabric the colour is much more intense and the colour overlays more highly defined. For this reason it is most important always to commence work by making a series of samples on pieces of scrap material before attempting a more complex design. These samples, no matter how small, help the artist to get the feel of the process and also explore the variety of effects which can be achieved by over-printing and cutting out the design motifs. From my own experience I have found that if this experimental work is not first carried out the resulting designs are usually inhibited.

Another basic reason for starting in this way is to make sure the iron,

The original transfer crayons developed by Binney and Smith (Europe) Ltd. The crayons which utilise the basic principles of sublistatic printing were first shown on the BBC's *Tomorrow's World* programme

Opposite The commercial packaging for transfer crayons, currently available in the USA. The illustration shows a display container which holds two dozen eight crayon packets. This product is marketed by Binney and Smith of New York

An exercise in colour mixing using transfer crayons. By completing this simple experiment the student is able to see exactly what combination of colours creates the various secondary shades. Rubbings incorporated into this type of work create many different results which are both physical and optical

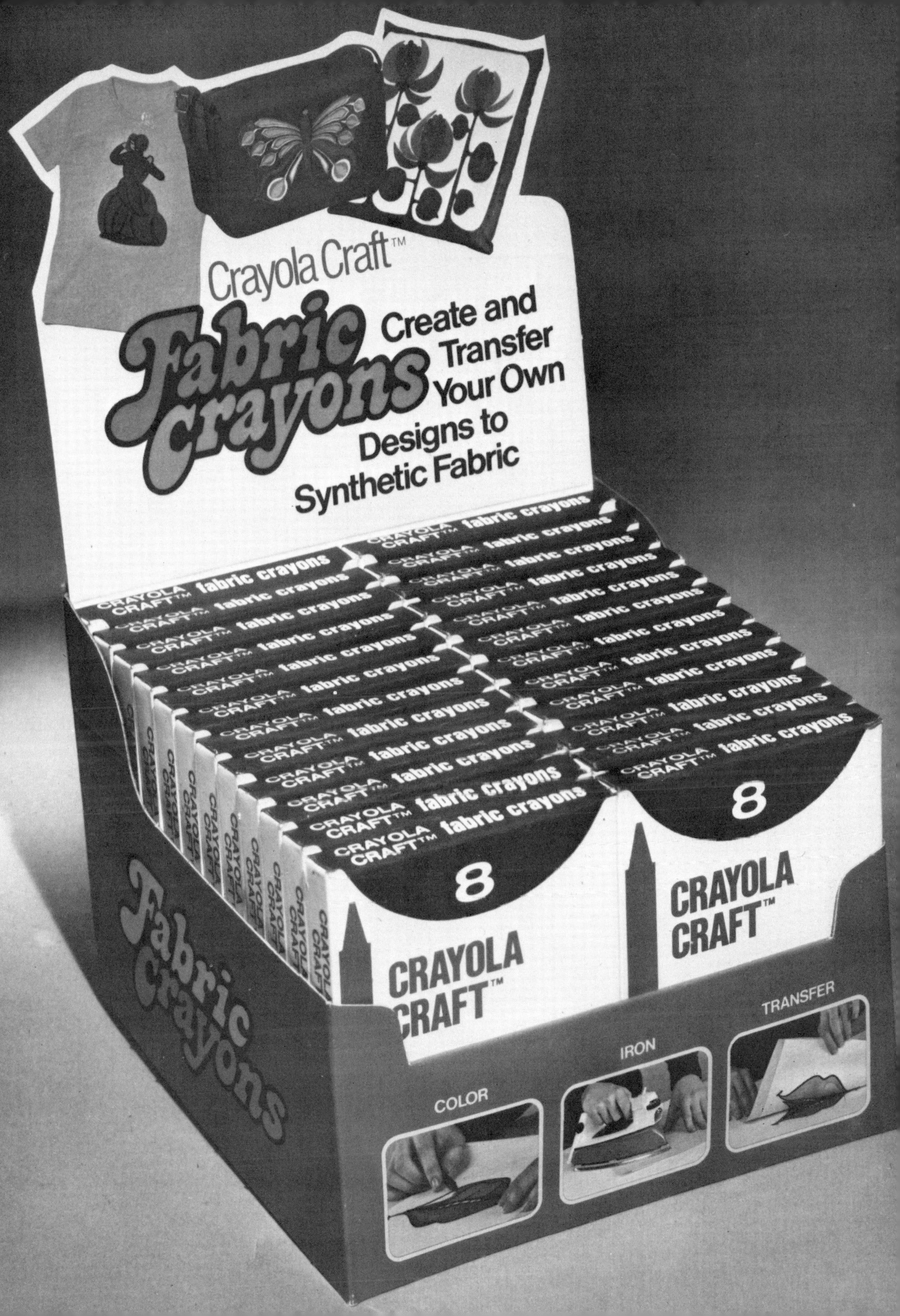
Crayola Craft™
Fabric Crayons
Create and Transfer Your Own Designs to Synthetic Fabric
CRAYOLA CRAFT™ fabric crayons
8
CRAYOLA CRAFT™
Fabric Crayons
COLOR
IRON
TRANSFER

A sophisticated dragon design by Peter Barker which shows the real potential of the transfer crayons. In the top illustration one sees the paper original and the resulting print. The panel opposite shows how the design can be reprinted to create an interesting composite design

or the press, is set at the correct temperature. In this type of work several charts should be made and transferred at slightly different temperatures for comparison. As we will see when discussing the transfer inks the hardness and type of bed on which one irons can also vary the intensity of the print; as can the paper type.

The choice of paper

As one can see from the illustrations, in all the examples, the design is first crayoned on paper before transfer. Any thin white drawing paper is suitable at this stage, although thick papers and thin tissue paper should be avoided for obvious reasons. If the design work is small, duplicating paper is ideal, as unlike the transfer inks the type of paper for use with the crayons is not too critical as the high colour loading allows a much wider tolerance. For the most satisfactory results onto thin nylon, where the dwell time is critical, a slightly glazed paper is recommended as this aids the speed of transfer.

NOTE. These initial recommendations for paper and fabrics, suitable for transfer printing, are deliberately non-specific, as one is concerned at this stage with the process as an art activity rather than a technical craft. For detailed specifications on paper types and fabric suitability in terms of industrial specifications see appropriate headings.

Suitable fabrics

As dealt with in great detail in the earlier chapter on fabric selection, transfer crayons only work on man-made fabrics, such as Terylene, Crimplene, Orlon, Tricel, Trevira and most nylons, which are of course commercially known trade names. One can therefore say, at this stage of working, that the transfer colours will only give a strong colour transfer, which is washable, onto this range of fabrics.

If they are used on natural fibres such as cotton, silk, wool or rayon (which is a wood base) the transfer is less intense and the colours not permanent. However these duller results are often ideal for starting embroideries or collage work and for this reason should not entirely be rejected.

Experimentation is the key to finding suitable materials and one will soon discover that cheap lining materials, nylon net and some mixtures are satisfactory, especially if the results are to be used for such activities as puppetry or drama. Likewise the simulated paper fabric, sold under the

trade name of Vilene, is suitable for transfer printing and is ideal for very modern experimental dresses or play clothes, as it is inexpensive.

Finally, for the most brilliant colours transfer the design onto a white or pale pastel fabric. However, in the experimental stages, do experiment with darker backgrounds as some of the results can be subtle and interesting.

Transferring the design

As the basic method of designing is mechanically simple, it becomes even more important that the design is transferred most carefully, as it soon becomes obvious that the relative success of the transfer design is directly related to the care with which one carries out the simple transfer procedure.

Listed below are the main points to consider when making a transfer print.

NOTE For all these early experiments a simple domestic electric flat iron is used, although a steam iron would not be switched to steam as this is unnecessary. If a steam iron is used care must be taken to ensure that the iron is moved continuously as the pattern on the sole of the iron would appear on the design if used on one area only.

Method of working

1 Select the type of fabric to be used, one which you have already tested.
2 Create your design on paper, blowing any small pieces of crayon, off the surface as these will print. For a really clean edged design cut out the image very carefully.
3 Prepare a 'bed' for ironing, by covering the table with several sheets of newspaper and a final sheet of clean paper to create a bed which is both clean and slightly soft.
4 Set iron to 'Cotton' heat. An ideal test for an iron is one of time. If the design prints in 10 seconds the iron is too hot, and if no image appears after 30 seconds the iron is too cool. Remember excessive heat will spoil the fabric.
5 Lay the fabric on the bed and then lay the paper design face down onto the fabric. Cover with a second sheet of paper to protect fabric from the direct heat of the iron.
6 Iron steadily over each area of the design for approximately 30 seconds or until transfer has taken place.
7 Before removing paper carefully lift corner of design to check colour strength. If not bright enough replace paper and iron a little longer. So that design does not move keep the iron on other corner of design, whilst checking colour strength.
8 When transferred to your satisfaction remove paper and the original design will have been transferred in reverse onto the fabric. No further processing is required and the design is now colour fast to washing.

NOTE That the feel of the fabric has not been affected by the dyes, unlike many conventional print processes (or the 'hot melt' process of transferring images mentioned in the introduction).

As is soon appreciated, the basic method of creating a design onto fabric is simple and relatively quick. One therefore sees how the artist can immediately begin to explore the many ways of extending his designs without the need of additional expensive equipment.

The original paper design showing how carefully the image must be cut out if a detailed result is required

Three designs by primary school children which show how the transfer crayons can be used as a logical development from the children's other pictorial work

The initial drawing. Design by Peter Barker

The design is carefully cut out

The transfer bed is prepared and the design carefully laid down

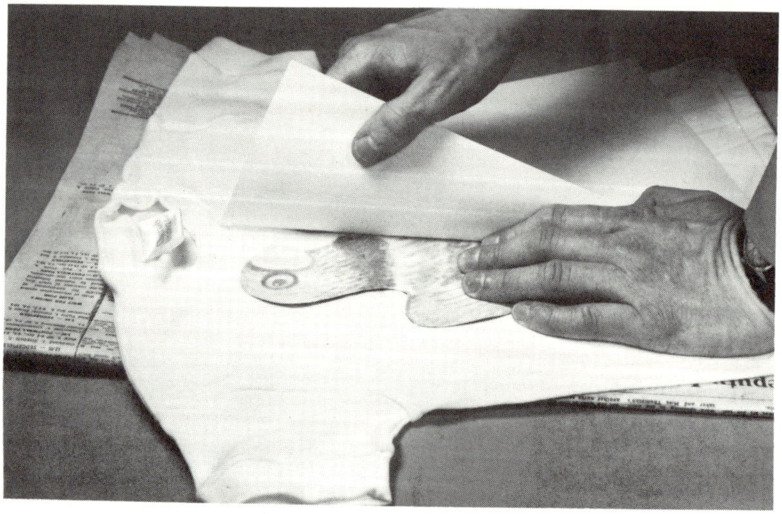

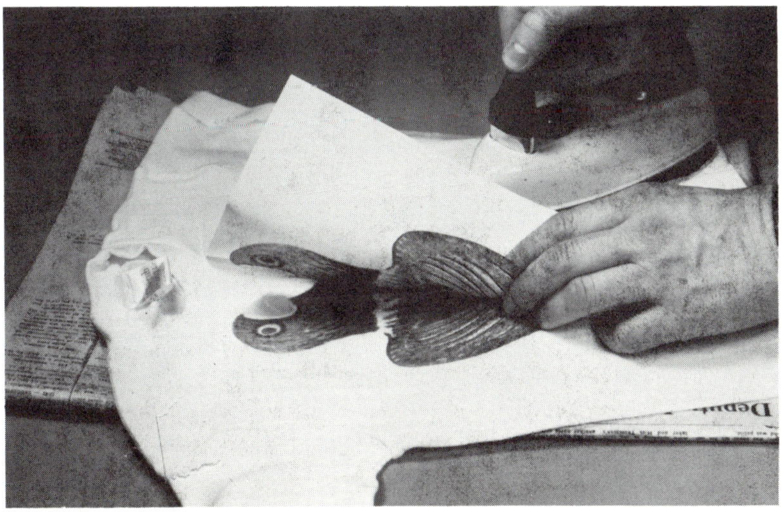

The transfer process using a domestic iron. In this illustration the designer is carefully assessing the colour strength on each area of the design

The completed design

The process of working for a complex non-figurative design. As in the design of the bird, after the drawing is completed, it has to be carefully cut out, to create a controlled edge. In this case a wider tolerance is acceptable as the design is to be printed many times

The bed is prepared and the design covered over so the iron does not mark the fabric

The initial design is then ironed carefully and checked at each stage to assess colour intensity

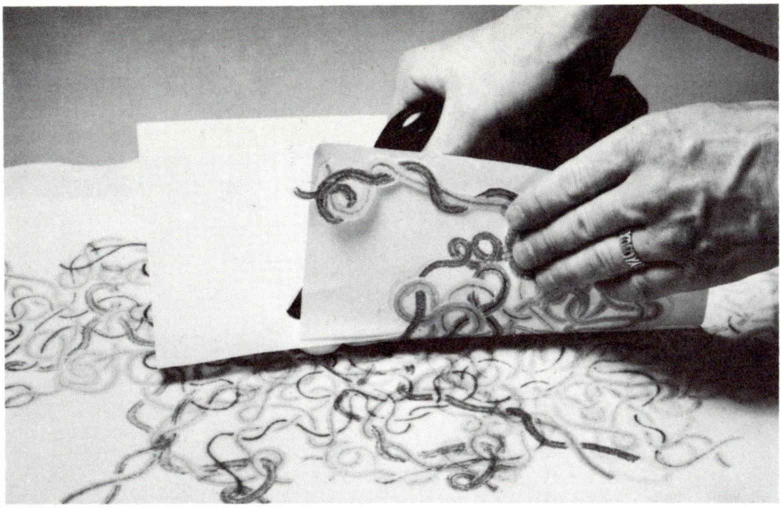

The image is used a number of times to create a multiple design

Where the design has become faint the designer can retouch the drawing before transferring again or use this fainter print to create a special image

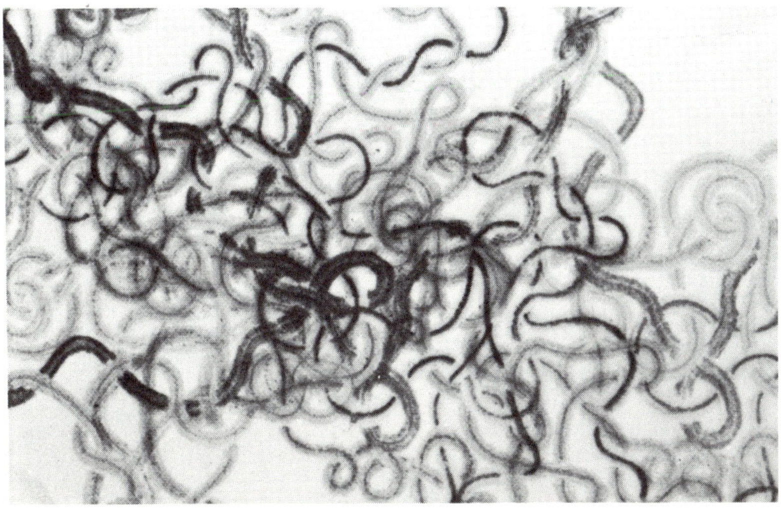

The completed design which uses the unique quality of the various parts to give it a three dimensional effect

The simple use of cut out shapes overlayed and printed

A series of printed textures and overprinted designs by Geraldine Knowles using transfer crayons. It is interesting to see how these free designs gradually become more figurative in form and develop into landscape and then become more abstract as the process is exploited

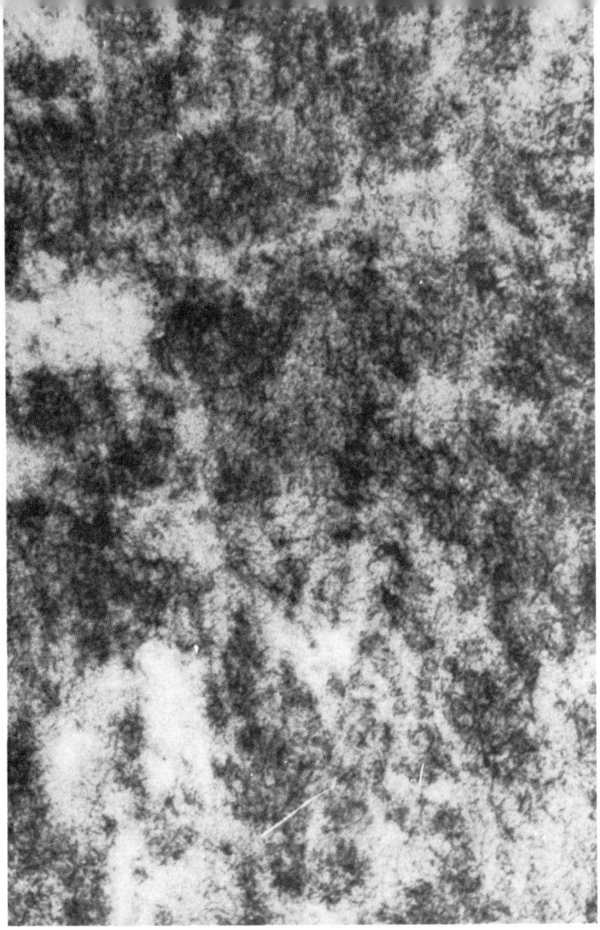

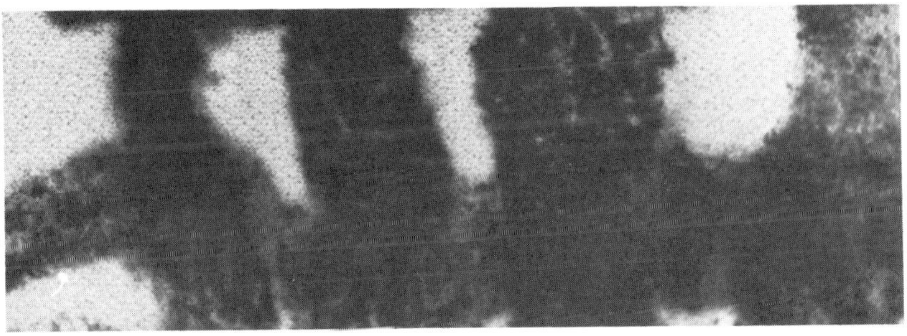

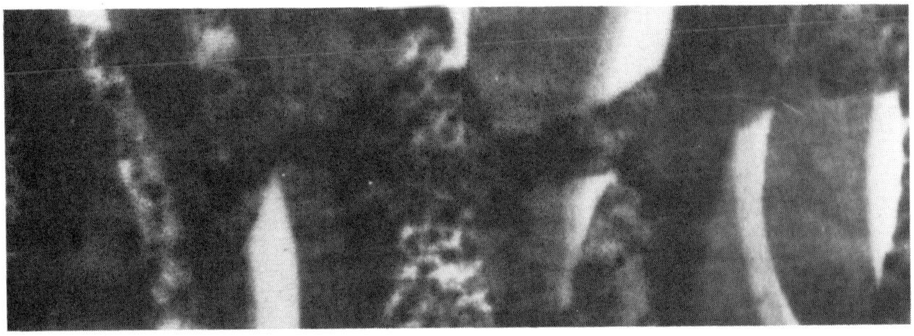

above left A printed rubbing

above right Rubbings and flat areas of colour cut up and overprinted

A single print created by working over a textured surface

A combination print using rubbings and flat areas together with second prints to produce lighter tones

A development from previous illustration

Stripes

Fragmented stripes vertical and horizontal

Fragmented stripes

Cut forms over textural grounds

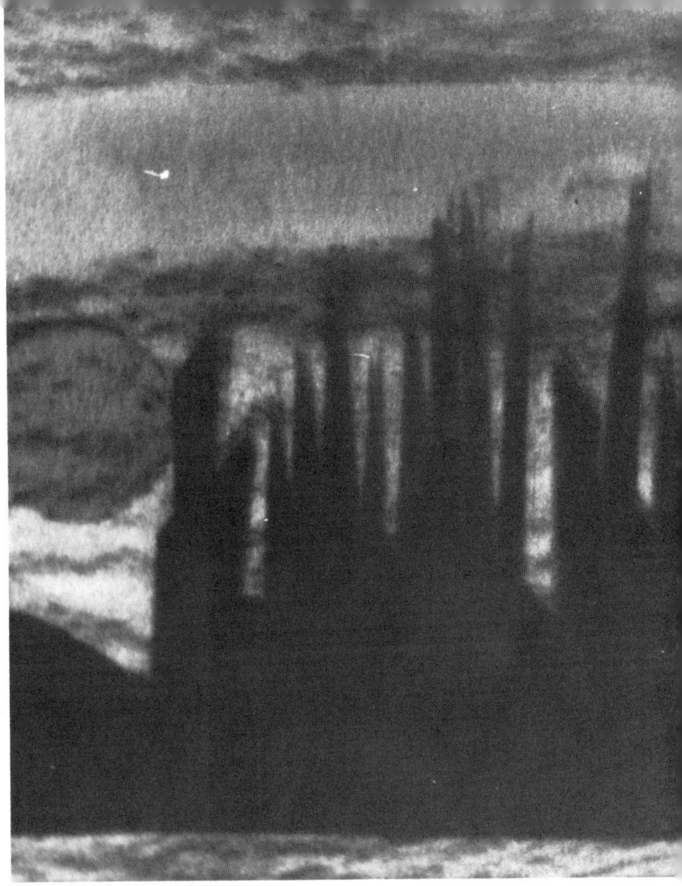

Series by Geraldine Knowles. An interesting series of designs which incorporate not only landscape but also introduce industrial shapes such as houses and masts. In turn these transfer printing designs became the starting point for a subsequent series of large scale embroideries

4 Extending the design from simple beginnings

As all the design work in transfer printing is first completed on to paper a great variety of figurative ideas as well as experimental collage work can be attempted and then transferred accurately on the chosen fabric. For example a free design could be cut out and then transferred, resulting in an image which has both spontaneity, as well as, a controlled outline.

Work with young children

In terms of work with young children it is this type of activity which, I feel, is most relevant. For if one says to children that the crayons are special fabric printing crayons one usually finds that the end results are tight and inhibited. However if the children are encouraged to draw simple patterns or figurative shapes, these can then be cut out and printed individually, or as a group frieze, incorporating overprinting and masked areas (see illustration below). For these early experiments Vilene is recommended as it is relatively inexpensive.

A large scale transfer printed mural measuring 182 cm × 60 cm (6 ft × 2 ft), produced by Class 5, Mousehold Avenue First School, Norwich

Young children should not handle a hot iron, so the teacher must do the ironing of these designs onto the fabric. I don't think this in any way inhibits the creative side of the work, as the ironing stage is only a mechanical process and in no way changes the quality of the initial drawing or design.

If one thinks logically of these ideas in terms of a progression, one can see how the pupil could first draw simple symmetrical forms which could then be transposed in a variety of ways. For example, circles could be drawn freely, cut out carefully and then overlayed to give an interesting combination of colours. In turn, the same shape could be explored by using sheets of texture, made up from rubbings of doileys, or other circular shapes, as we can see in the example on page 45. Likewise a whole variety of circular patterns could be cut out from sheets of melted crayon and then incorporated into a complicated design, using circles of one colour to create a contrast (see illustration on page 43).

As many of these collage techniques necessitate the use of a backing paper on which one first glues the paper shapes before transfer, it is important to remember that this backing paper should be quite thin (newsprint being ideal) and the glue should be a wallpaper type adhesive. As a thick backing paper and a PVA type glue would create all sorts of problems in terms of difficulty in transfer and adhesion onto the fabric itself. An adhesive additive is sometimes added to the ink to help overcome the problem of the paper moving during transfer. See chapter 8, page 110.

Simple ideas for picture making

What is particularly interesting when using transfer crayons with younger children, is that their ideas can so easily be developed both as exercises in pattern and as realistic pictures incorporating areas of texture. The illustration on page 46 shows how a simple striped pattern can be cut up to produce many different end results, and in the same way a drawing of a fish or a dragon can be exploded to produce a sophisticated design which could be easily developed into a collage embroidery. In terms of more figurative work one can see how different textures can be produced from rubbings, and then used as a background for figures, or as part of a composite design (see illustration on page 49).

In the same way brass rubbings and embossed surface rubbings can also be attempted using this method, although one must remember that designs incorporating lettering should be avoided as these areas would print in reverse. One project which immediately comes to mind when using small designs onto fabric is the creation of individual Christmas and greetings cards.

As transfer printing, at this stage, is used purely as an extension of the children's other work and indeed develops many of the drawing techniques they have already mastered, one can see how letter forms and number shapes can give them a whole wealth of ideas which can be developed onto fabric.

Lettering

If lettering is required as an integral part of a design or picture, it can be achieved simply by drawing the letter shapes with a ballpoint pen, reversing the paper and then colouring in the incised lines which will appear in reverse. If one cuts out these reversed letters this will also help the shapes to print more clearly.

However a more interesting technique which allows a greater amount of development is to first cut out the letters in thick drawing paper or thin card as positive forms, and then one lays these shapes on the fabric. If the letters are then covered with a sheet of solid colour, stripes or

A simple scribbled design which has been cut up in the paper state and re-pasted before transfer onto fabric

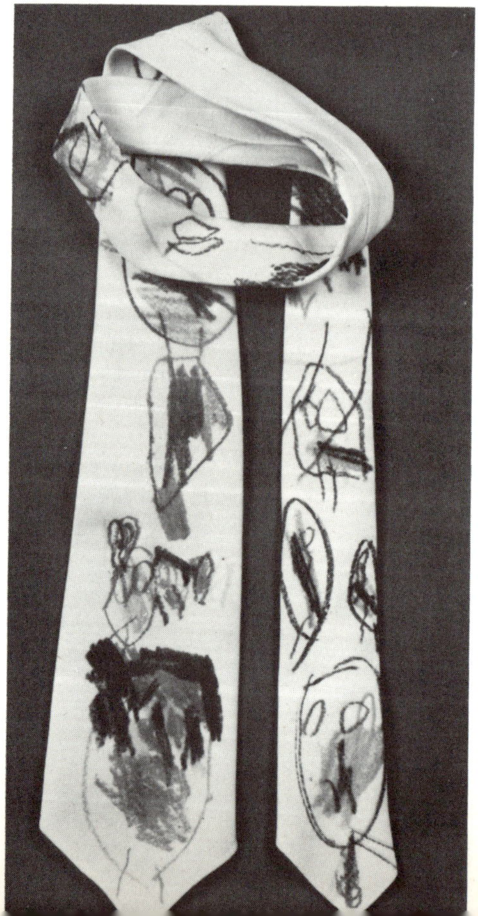

Owls by Adam aged 3½ years. Even at this age children can create designs using this technique, as the drawing process is simply an extension of conventional crayon drawing. The background is a white, commercially produced, crimplene tie

A simple hand shape used to start off a primary school project using transfer crayons

The small exhibition shows a number of different prints from the same design and also the original paper pattern which has been cut out

A group frieze incorporating areas of overlayed colour and also masked shapes. In this technique the animals and trees are first cut out of thick paper and layed onto the fabric before the background design is placed in position for printing

textures, and ironed, the letters will be masked out in white, with the colour printed, as the background. In the same technique the letters can be coloured, on the reverse side before being transferred, thus resulting in a coloured letter with a contrasting background.

This method of working is particularly useful when accurate lettering is required, ie for banners or theatrical work, as the letters can be cut out of strips of paper, thus ensuring that all the letters are of the same height.

The same technique can, of course, be used for figures, animals, birds, trees, flowers, etc, and we can see in the illustration of the *Jungle* on page 40 how a very interesting and complicated design can be achieved using this masking process. The idea of printing the background after the main images have been transferred is especially relevant when working with young children, as they naturally work in this way and consequently soon appreciate the necessity to cut out each shape before printing it onto fabric.

Another reason why one encourages the children to cut out their designs before transferring them, is that this simple method allows the artist to register the design accurately. Consequently, if, after the transfer, a small area has been missed, which can happen, no matter how carefully one works, the mistake can easily be rectified by replacing the paper on the incomplete design and ironing over the offending area for a little longer. In other words this method of working stops the process from becoming a one off, hit or miss, technique which is the failing of so many fabric printing activities.

As discovered during the experimental stages, transfer printed designs can be printed a number of times, but the image gradually becomes fainter, due to the loss of dye colour. However this characteristic can be used to advantage, especially for figurative work. For example, a group of flowers and plants, in a garden scene, would certainly become more interesting in spacial terms, if the paper shapes were printed a number of times individually and as masked overprints. Likewise a group of figures could take on a new dimension, if some of the people were printed in the background, with the brightly coloured first prints masked off in the foreground.

Graphic techniques using transfer crayons

Techniques, in any art form, can always be criticised if they dominate the creative process, but one sees in transfer printing, as in many craft activities, how the introduction of new ways of working often helps to maintain the student's interest and helps him develop his designs in different ways. This is certainly true in the case of the two techniques discussed below, as one gives the student a controlled line and the other allows a more versatile coloration to be achieved. It is also interesting to note that both these techniques were originally developed for use with conventional wax crayons and therefore might already be familiar to students.

Chalk and crayon

As is quickly evident when working with transfer crayons, their very nature does not allow a fine line to be achieved no matter how carefully the crayon is sharpened. Obviously this working characteristic is desirable as the student develops his ideas into more controlled images. The method illustrated on page 56 shows how it can be achieved by first apply-

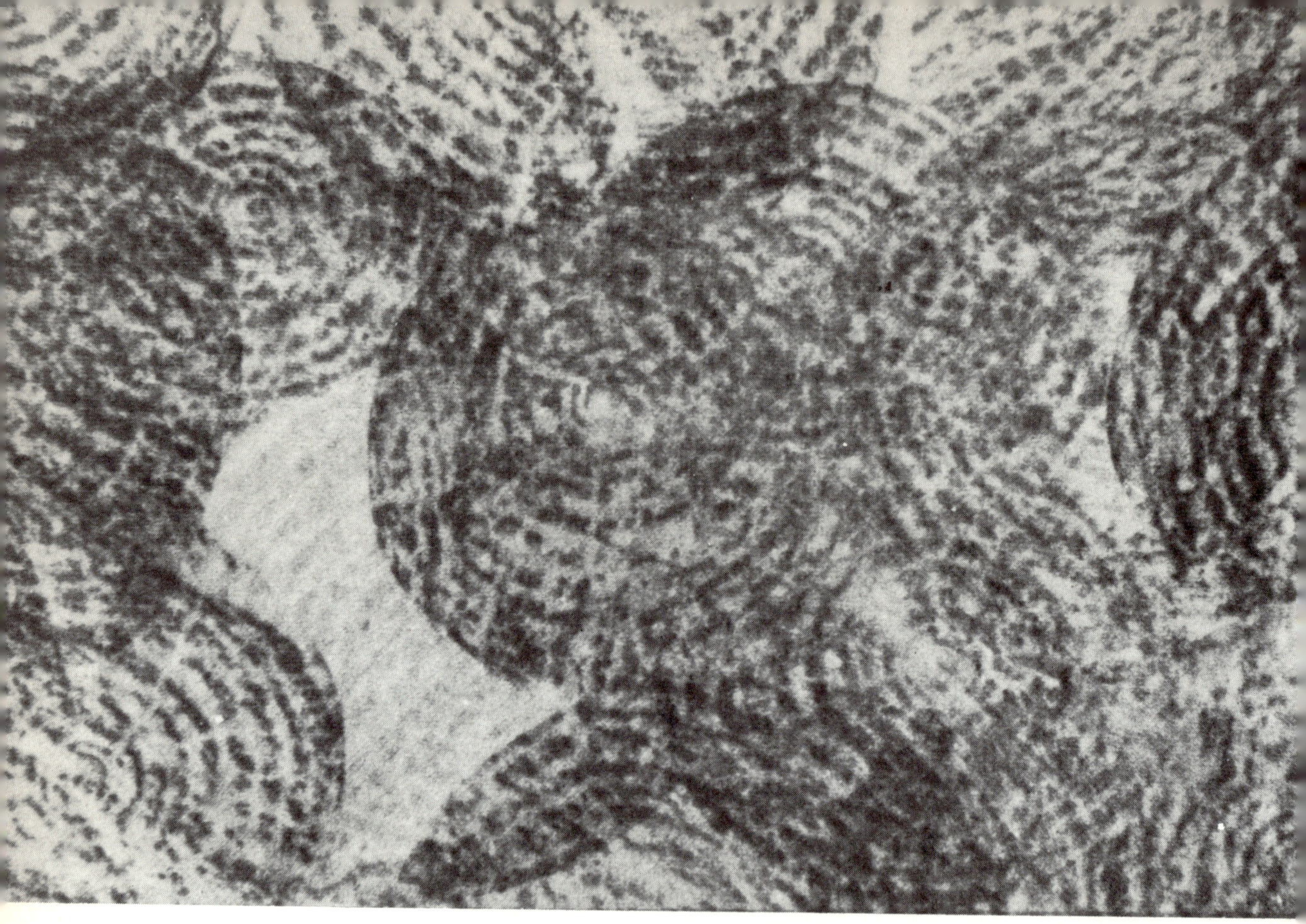

Detail of a circular design produced from rubbings

The original paper shapes crayoned in contrasting colours. As one can see the rubbings were first produced and then cut out. In this work the pieces of paper left behind are often interesting and could be used for another design

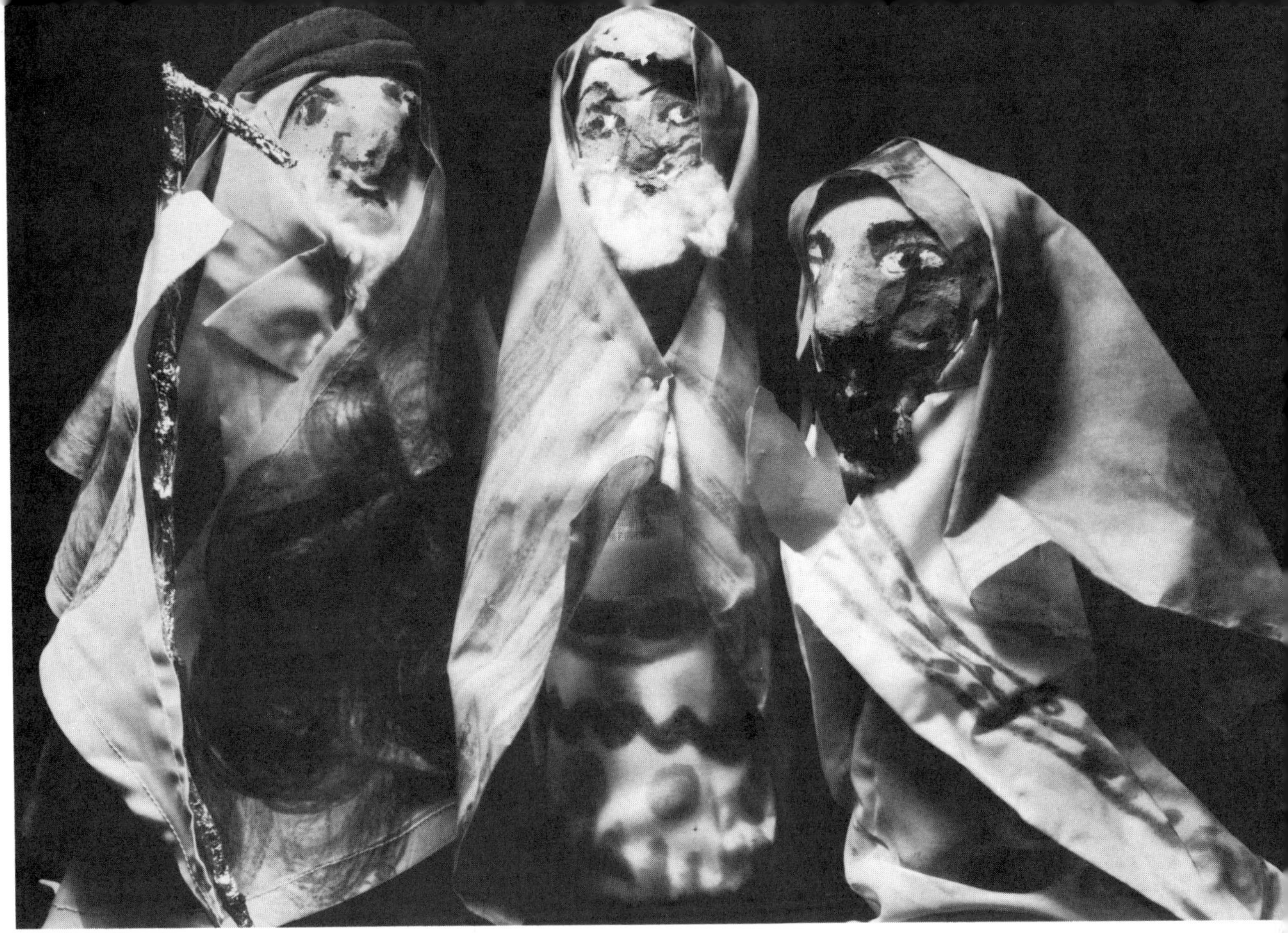

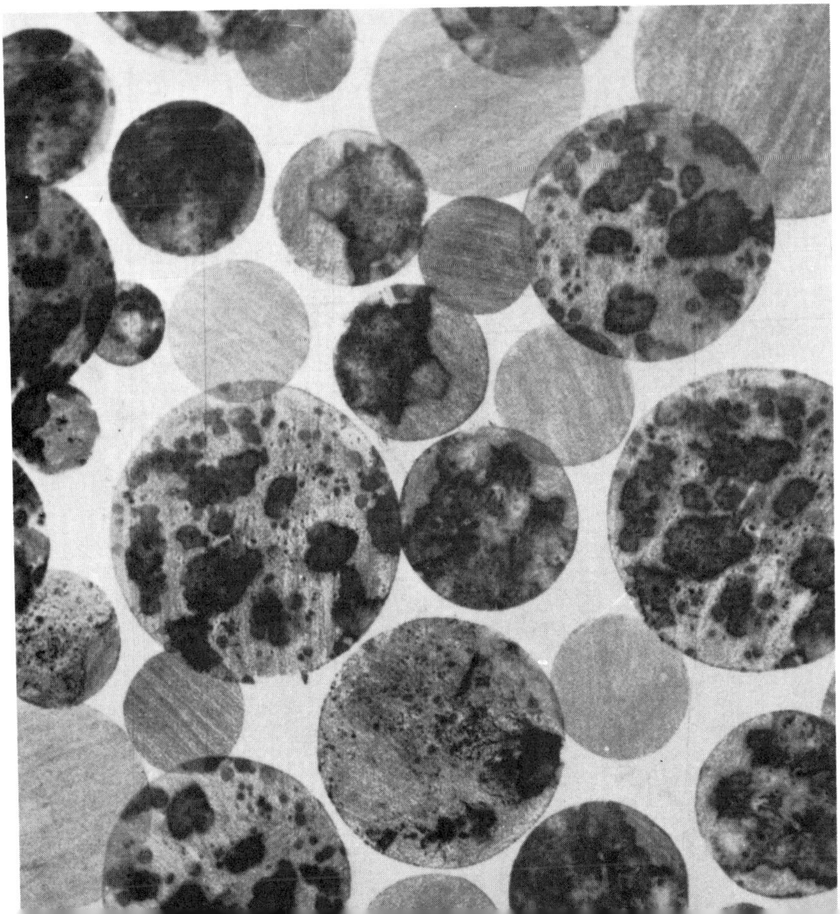

The Three Kings. Simple transfer printed designs have been used to create the costumes for these Nativity puppet figures
Mousehold Avenue First School, Norwich

A highly colourful design produced by melting transfer crayons and then cutting out the resulting blobbed designs. For contrast simple circles produced from a single colour have been used in the background

ing chalk onto a sheet of paper which is then covered with a thick coating of crayon, creating a type of carbon paper. When a second sheet is laid over the crayon a fine draying can be produced simply by incising a line into the top sheet, using a ballpoint pen: the image being picked up on the reverse side of the top paper as a negative, with the line cut out as a positive in the chalk and crayon layer beneath. Both images can be printed and if a positive image is required in linear form the drawing should be completed on the back of the original sheet. One can see this method of working being particularly applicable for *art nouveau* type designs and for over-printing detail over solid areas of colour.

Melted crayon designs

As one would expect the wax content of the crayons allows them to be easily melted and as we know from using ordinary wax crayons this allows many different graphic techniques to be explored. The added bonus being that whatever effects are produced on paper can now be accurately translated onto fabric.

The simplest way of introducing this way of working, is to scrape a few small pieces of wax from the different crayons and then place them between a sandwich of paper before ironing them together with an iron at a low temperature. This fuses the colours together and produces a fascinating double image. Both pieces of paper can now be used and either

A curtain produced from rubbings from plastic doylies

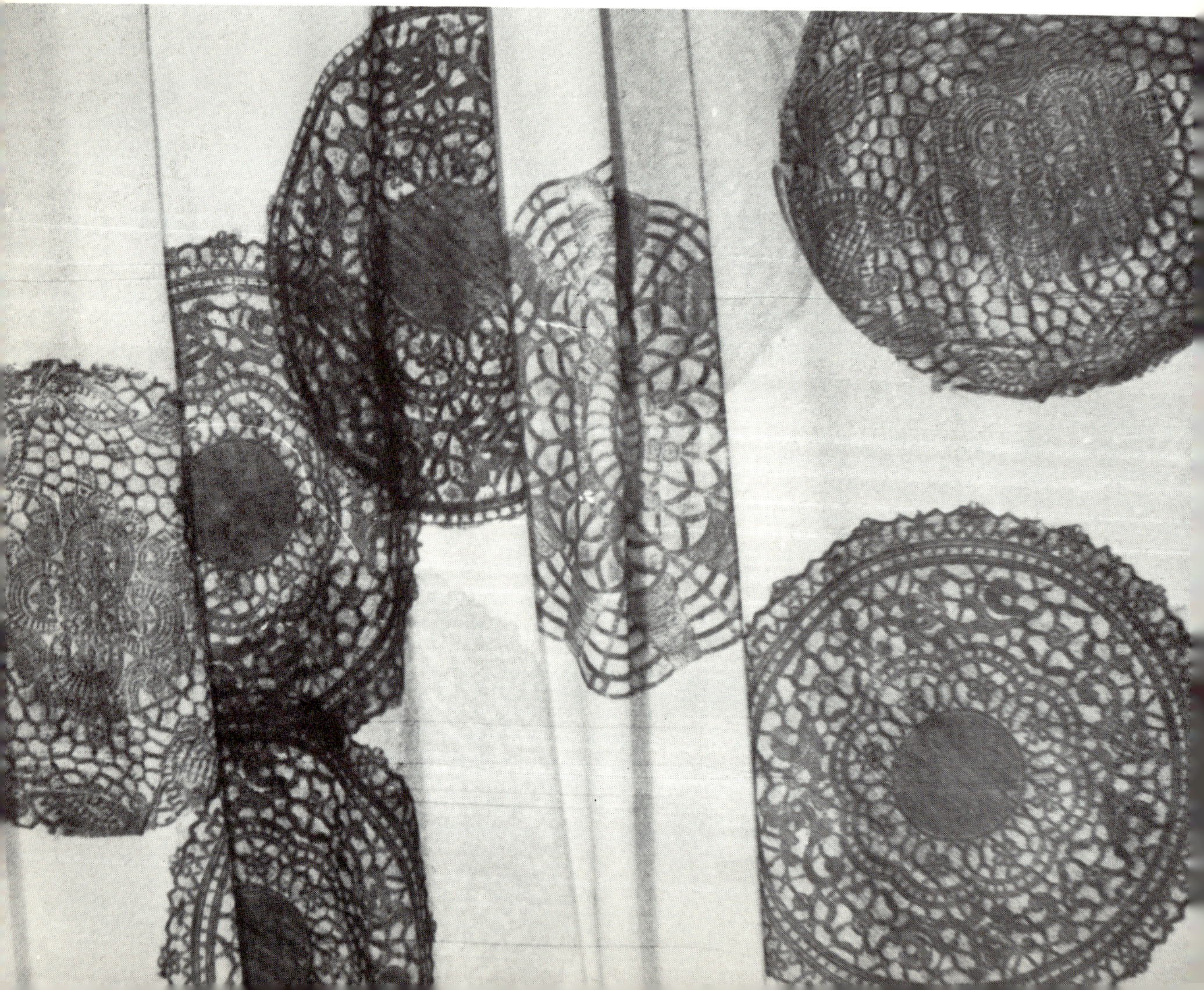

transferred direct or cut out into geometric shapes or parts of a figurative design. The resulting prints are always interesting and the thickness of the wax on the paper allows one to produce a number of prints from each original. As an extension of this type of work, pieces of transfer crayon can be melted (in a bun tin), and then painted onto the paper in broad brush strokes of heavy impasto. If the resulting designs are to be transferred onto a garment care should be taken to ensure that the design does not print the back of the garment, as one is using a heavily impregnated sheet of paper, which will transfer very quickly.

Still using heat, a more sophisticated result can be achieved by warming the paper by ironing before one commences to draw. This method slightly softens the crayon and so produces a subtle line, similar to a pastel chalk.

It is interesting to note at this stage that for some experimental work the crayons can be used straight onto the fabric and then ironed, but as one would expect the results are not accurate and give a rather insensitive line, as it is obviously difficult to work directly onto fabric unless it is stiff. However this method of working could be used as the starting point for collage work.

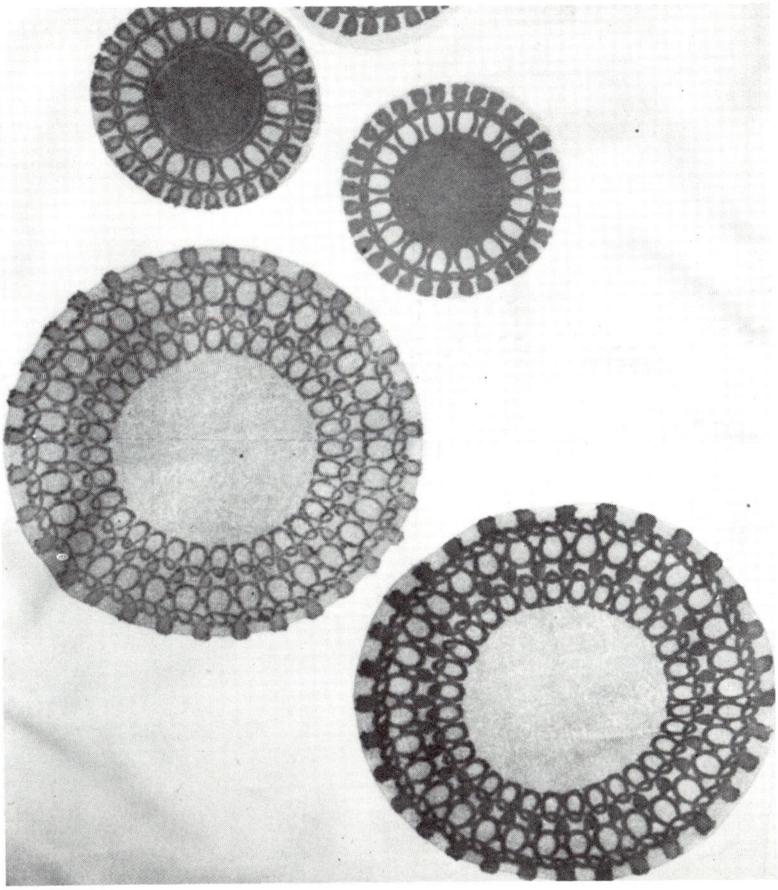

In this design, which was used to decorate a shoe-bag, rubbings from different types of paper doylies have been used in a variety of ways, some over circles of colour and others used as negative masked shapes printing the solid colour through the doiley which is used as a stencil

A small fish motif created from sheets of melted and crayoned colour. The sea weed was then added as an overprint

Below In this illustration a multicoloured striped design has been cut up and mounted on a backing paper before being transferred

Below right The resulting design printed onto Bondina

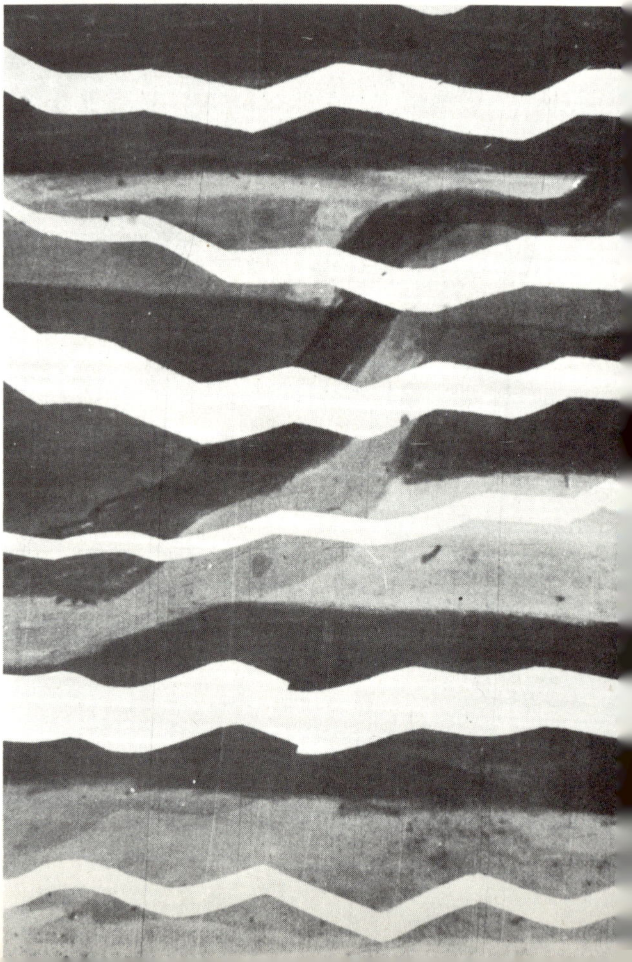

Various patterns created from stripes of colour. This type of work is so simple that it can be attempted by the youngest child

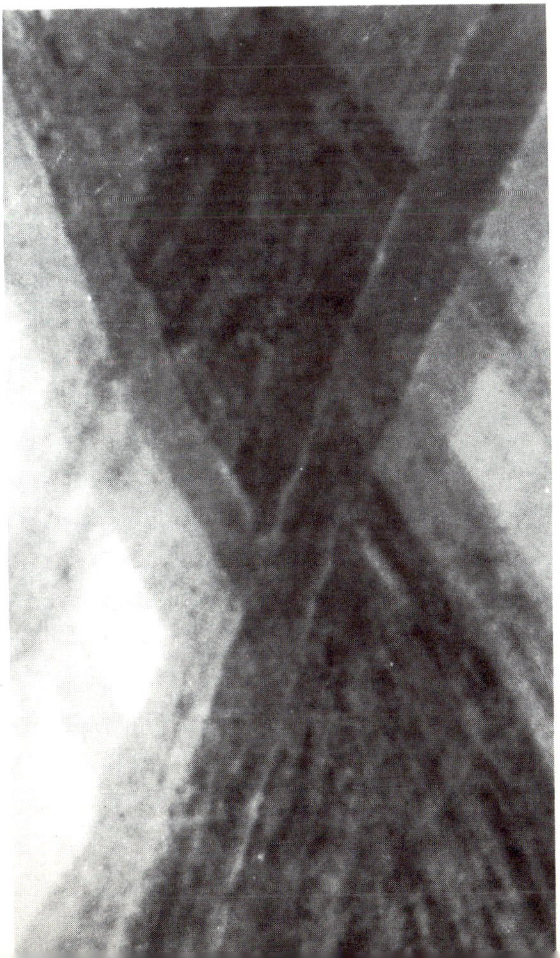

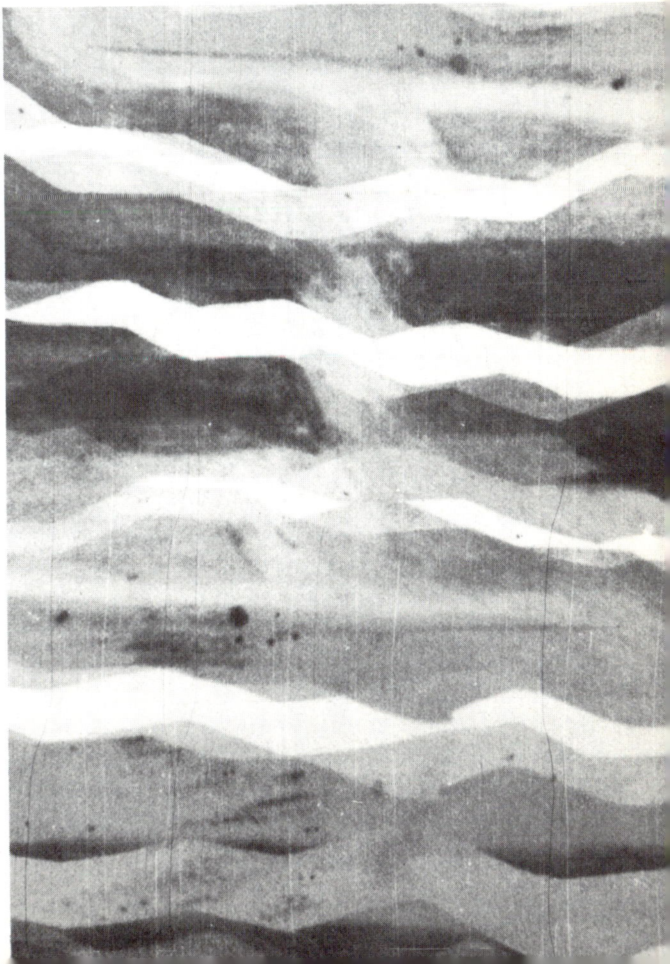

A shark created from one page of crayoned patterns which have been cut up and rearranged

A fanciful dragon produced in the same way as the shark, but in this case a more formal striped pattern was used as the background paper

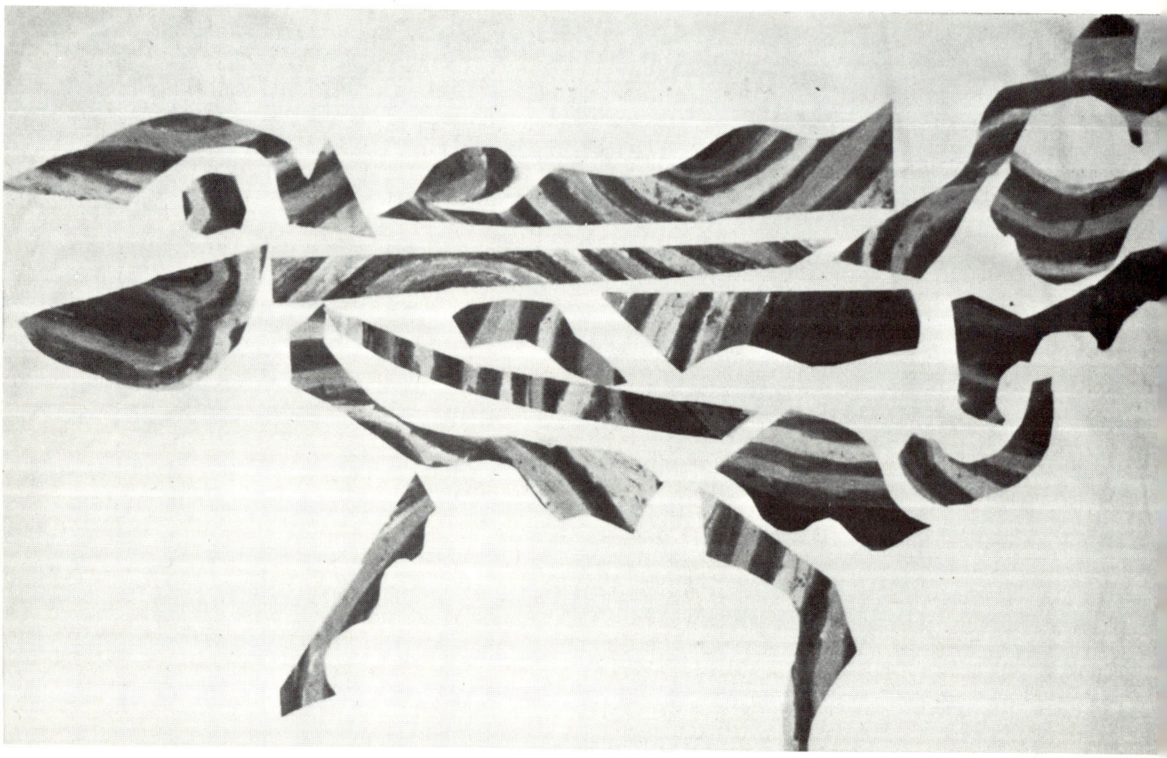

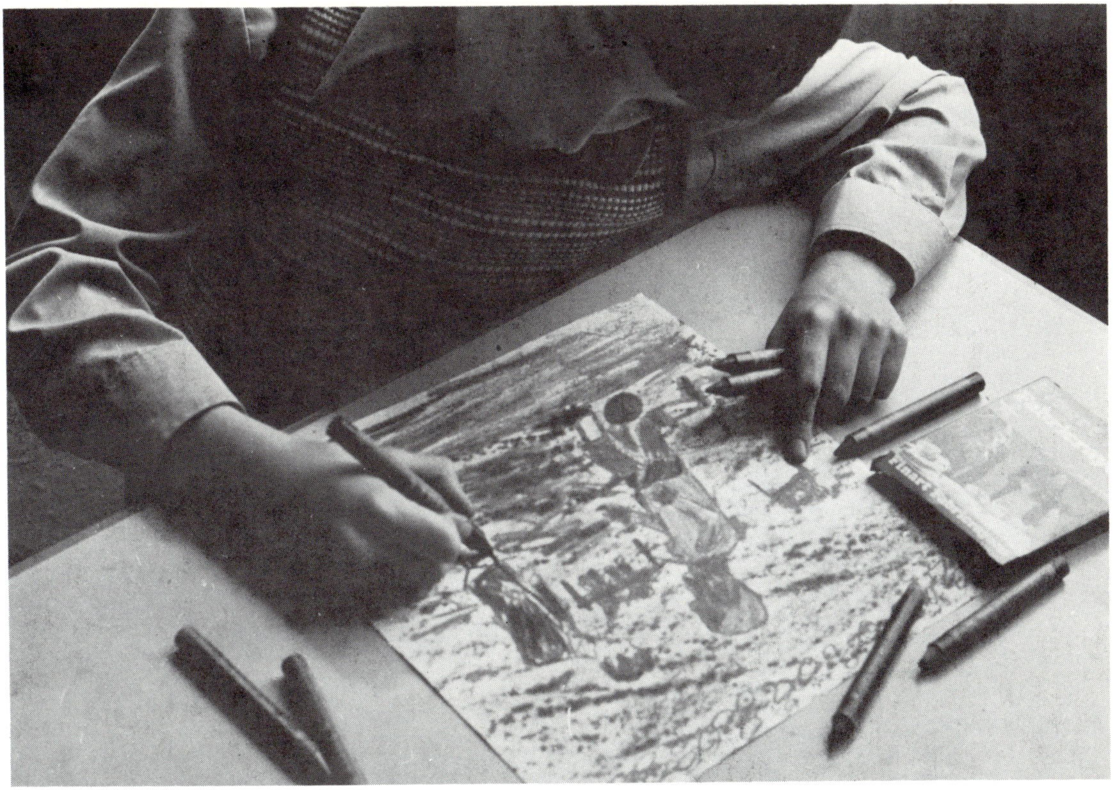

An interesting way of using rubbings as the background for a football match picture

An intricate design evolved from the child's own name. In all this work the transfer crayons are used as a development from the children's other pattern work and not as a special activity completed in isolation

A child's name made up from positive and negative shapes which have been carefully rearranged to create the final design. In this type of work the paper design work is emphasised as the final transfer on to fabric faithfully reproduces the original pattern

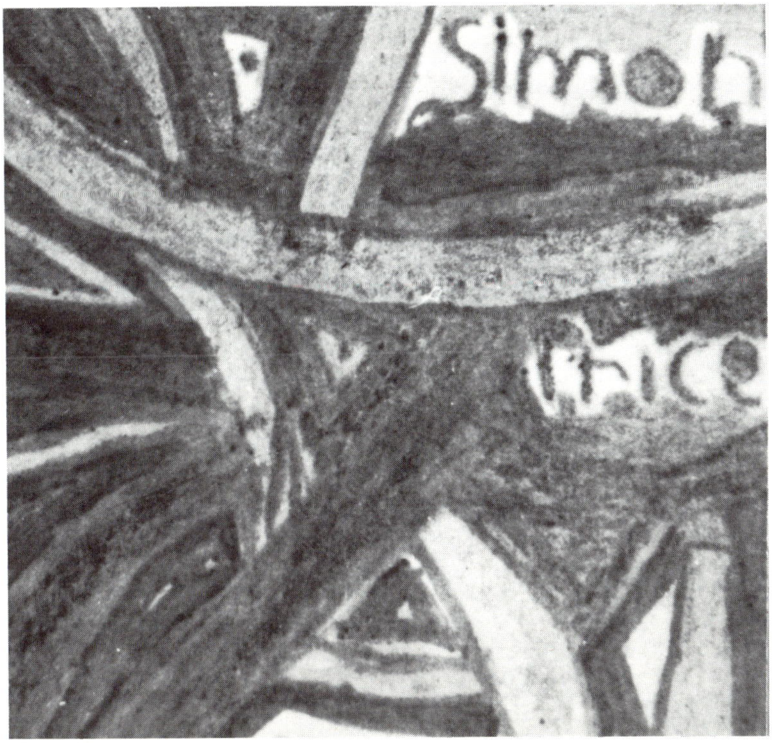

A pattern incorporating stripes and letters

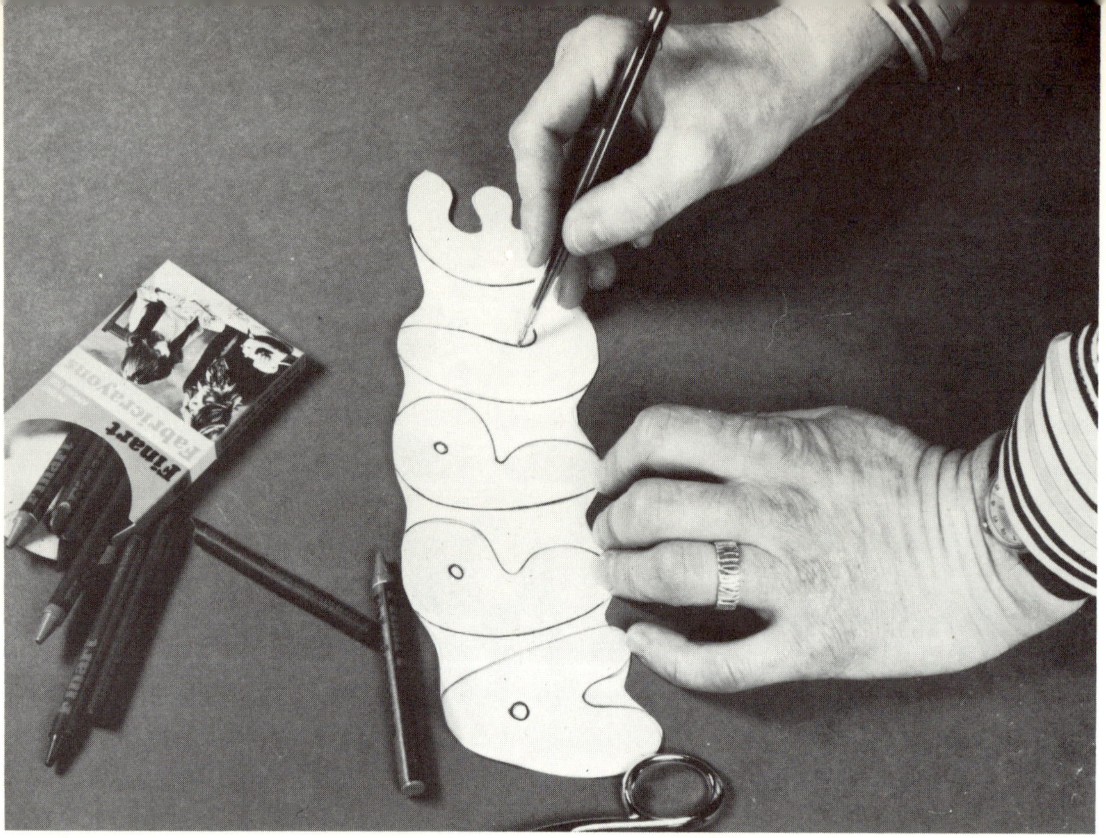

One way of lettering. In this technique the letters are drawn heavily in a ballpoint and then coloured in on the reverse side

As far as possible the letters should be cut out for clarity and to keep the design as clear as possible

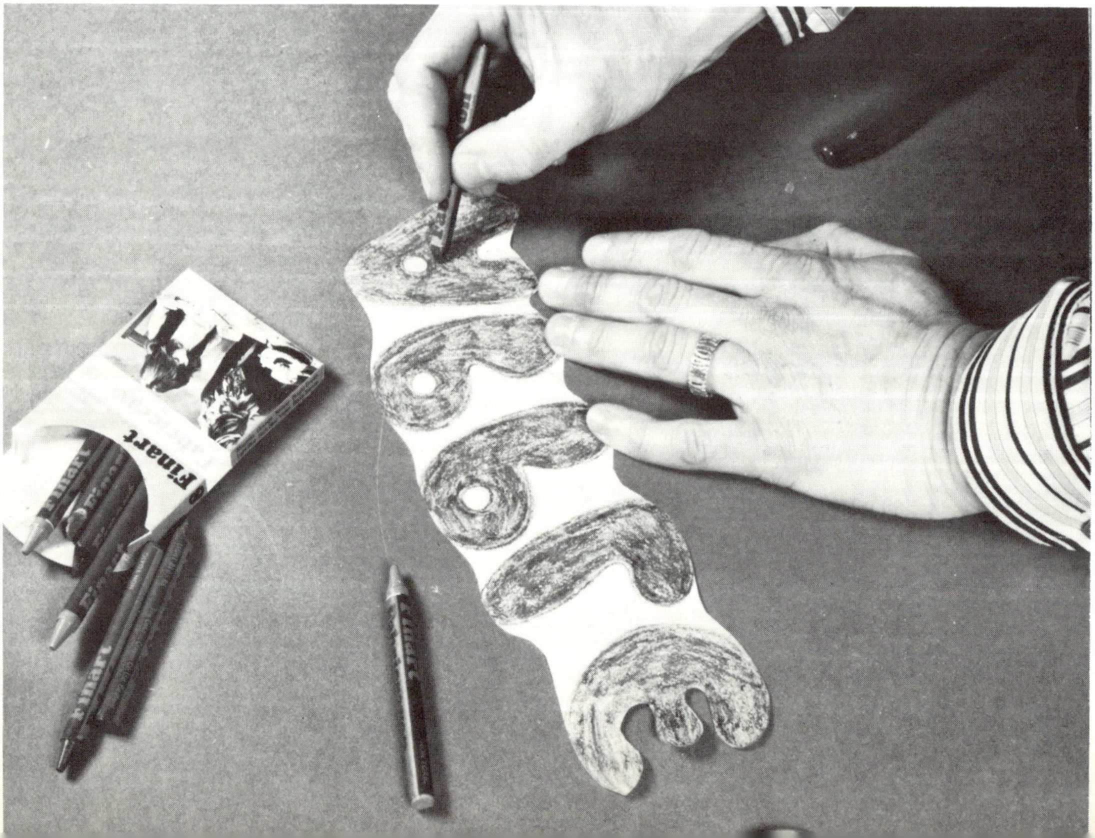

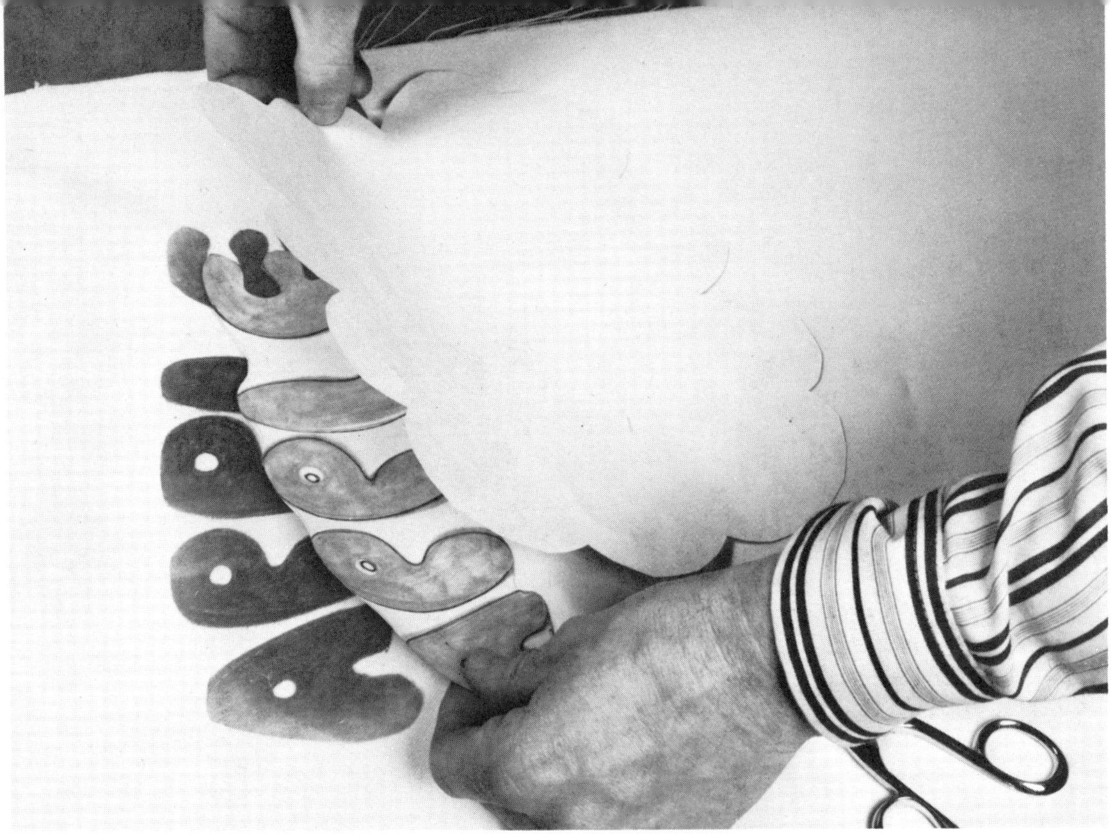

If a background is required a second sheet can be created and either printed with the lettering or afterwards, as shown here. This method does allow you to check the clarity of the lettering before adding the background

As shown on the right of this sample, a more sophisticated result is obtained by cutting the letter forms out before transfer and then using them as a mask under a larger coloured background sheet. This method is ideal for banners and tee-shirts, etc, where a very clear line is required

This series illustrates how to create a background behind a number of detailed foreground shapes. The clowns were first cut out very carefully and transferred. The paper clowns were then replaced and the foreground shapes placed over them

Opposite The finished design with the detailed background appearing in the shapes behind the clowns. See also colour plate facing page 120

A simple test to show the gradual decrease of colour when the initial design is printed a number of times

A chalk and transfer crayon technique used to create fine detail. In this initial stage the transfer colours are applied thickly over a layer of chalk

Another sheet of plain paper is then placed over the crayon and the design drawn into the back of the top sheet with a ballpoint pen

The pressure of the pen picks up the crayon onto the back of the top sheet and the shape design in a negative form is left etched in the original chalk and crayon layer. Both papers can be printed with interesting results

Detailed pop images showing the versatility of the crayon and chalk transfer technique Designs by Frank Birtwhistle

Melted crayon technique. Different effects can be obtained by melting the transfer crayons between a sandwich of paper

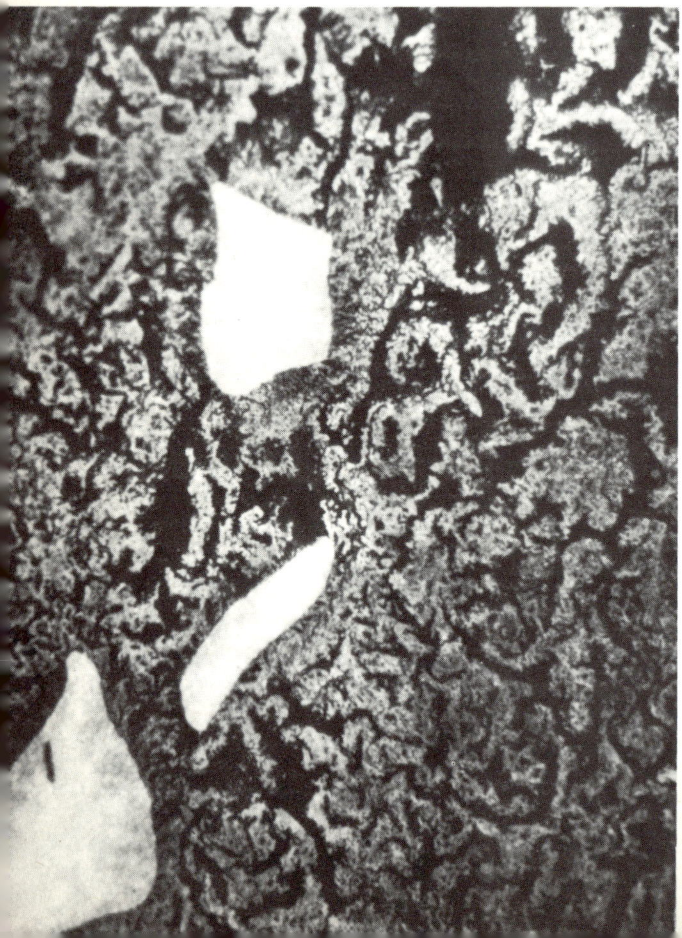

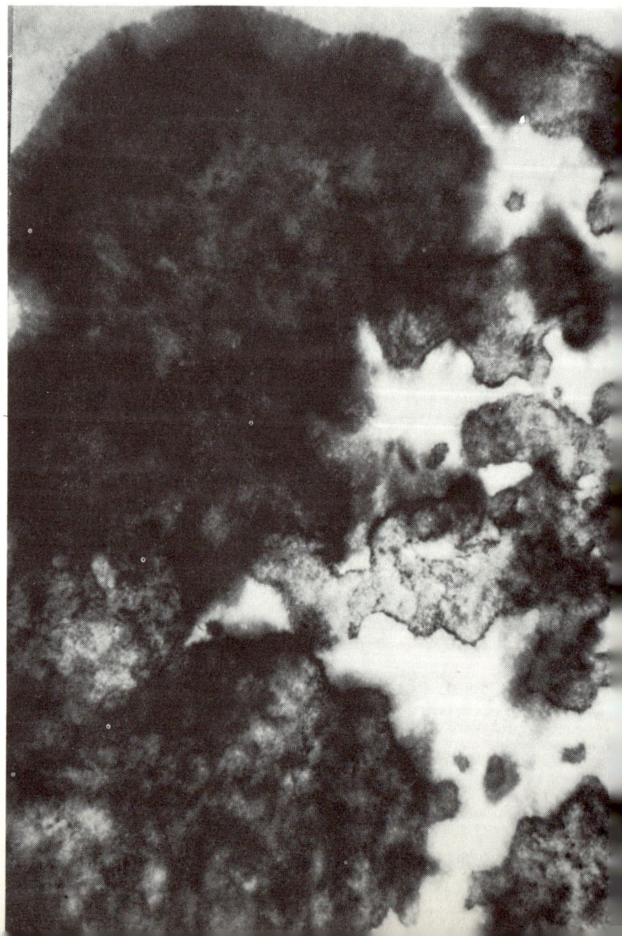

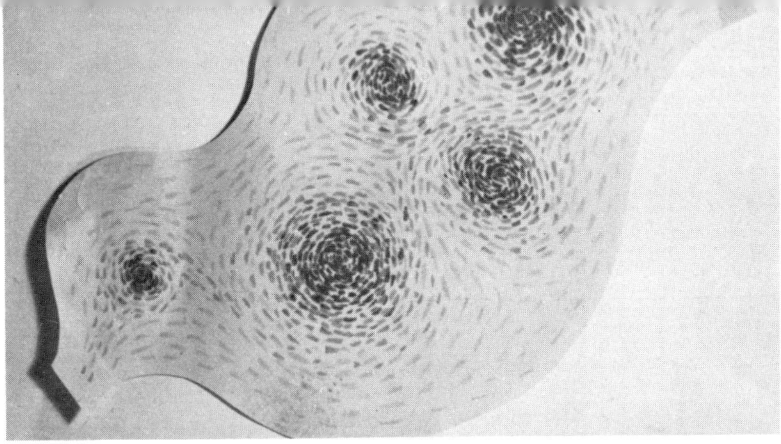

A flowing rhythmic design from small dots and dashes

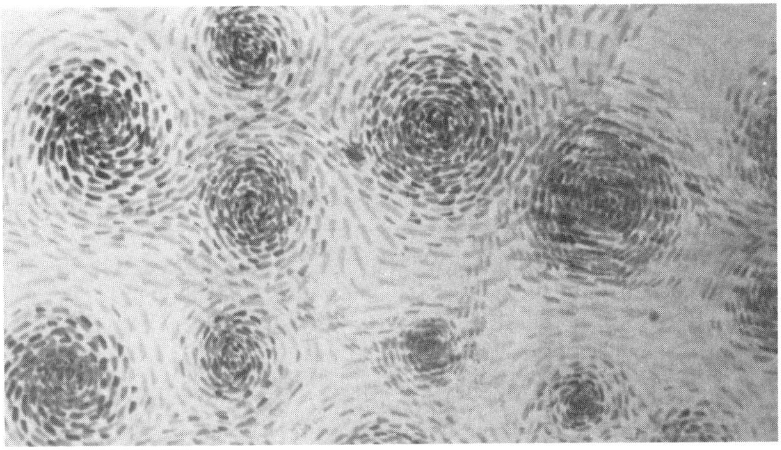

The final design created by overprinting the initial motif again and again. Design by Peter Barker

A geometric design in transfer crayons using a limited range of colours. In this type of work the design is carefully drawn out in pencil before being coloured, as the pencil lines do not show on the final print

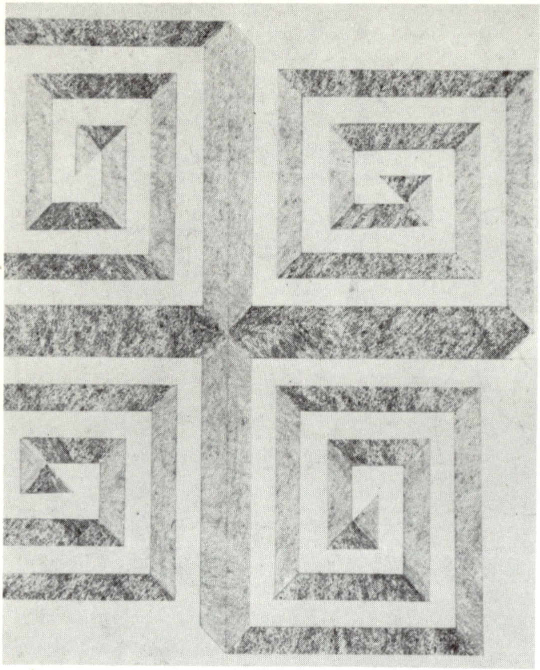

A series of complex geometric designs by Peter Barker. In all these examples the artist first draws up the design very accurately and then marks each piece before cutting the shapes out with a sharp knife.

Each piece is then coloured and the final design mounted onto a thin backing paper using double-sided tape before being transferred

All these examples were created specifically for decorating highly personalised dresses where one motif was used to give emphasis to one panel of the garment

5 Transfer inks

As mentioned in the Introduction of the book, transfer colours can be applied to the paper by means of inks, or the transfer crayons which have already been discussed. Although the crayons have enormous potential in terms of producing individual fabric designs, it is the inks or transfer dyes which one feels could eventually dominate this way of working in secondary schools and colleges, as they already have in many areas of industrial textile printing.

At the moment the distribution of transfer inks for educational use is somewhat limited. However, a set of twelve colours suitable for the designer is readily available. In addition a number of commercial ink manufacturers are willing to supply transfer inks, in quantities suitable for use in colleges and schools, together with the appropriate thinning agents and extenders (see suppliers on page 140).

NOTE The designer's colours mentioned above are water based, as are the Sublaprint 70600 screen printing paste colours and the Dispersol range of dyes, whereas the other transfer colours listed are spirit based and are consequently thinned with white spirit or specially formulated thinners.

The great potential of using the inks is their flexibility, as the colour can be applied to the paper by brush, roller, printing blocks and of course by screen, and if the water-based inks are used in combination with the crayons some very exciting resist effects can be achieved.

At this stage the technique for working and the eventual transfer method is similar to using the transfer crayons. However, as more sophisticated results are required a detailed appraisal of printing techniques have to be studied and these considerations will be dealt with later in this chapter. As in the case of the crayons, if a student is given too much technical information at the beginning of the project it is inevitable that the resulting designs are too inhibited.

I therefore recommend that the study of transfer inks is started by preparing a large number of papers (using duplicating paper) which explore the inks showing as many textural effects as possible. Starting with plain sheets of colour the student could then produce blob prints, splatter patterns, string prints, roller prints and block prints using all types of found shapes, and experimental line effects using different drawing tools.

If each texture is completed on a different sheet of paper, or the colours used are isolated into different ranges, onto different papers, the student is then in a position to complete a whole series of simple collage experiments, as we can see from the examples illustrated on pages 67 and 78.

If the students have already completed some transfer printed experiments using the crayons, they will obviously be aware of the colour change which occurs from paper onto fabric, after transfer. However, as the inks do emphasize this colour change even further, it is important to fully appreciate these chromatic differences, and for this reason a range of simple colour charts, onto different fabrics and using different papers, would be of great use. As one is repeatedly emphasizing the use of colour charts, each student should be encouraged to keep a spring backed folder, so that none of these experimental sheets and fabric examples are lost, especially if this work is being considered for examinations.

To summarise the potential of the transfer inks, these can be listed as follows:

1 Colour can be applied to paper by brushes, printing, paint rollers, screens, etc by varying the consistancy of the colour.
2 Inks can be used in combination with crayons to achieve interesting resist effects.
3 If used in a collage technique one can make last minute additions prior to printing or add areas of colour or texture as the work progresses.
4 Good sharp edges to colour boundaries can be achieved by cutting the paper.
5 Large areas of single colour can be achieved by screening and these can be used to imitate dyed backgrounds.
6 Many copies of a single unit can be made by screen or block and then assembled into a more complex design. This method is useful when assessing different design arrangements ie half drop, full drop, half step (brick pattern), before committing design onto the final fabric.
7 Inks can be used directly onto fabric if it is pre-washed, but during fixing with iron or press, design should be still sandwiched between paper. Finally the print should be washed in lukewarm soapy water to remove excess thickener from fabric.
8 A disadvantage (or to be deliberately exploited) is the shrinkage of very thin paper such as newsprint, which leads to cockling after the aqueous inks have been applied. When flattened under iron, or press, during transfer operation an additional patterned effect occurs within the solid areas. This can be minimised by pre-wetting and stretching the paper, or using a slightly heavier quality if extremes of accuracy are required. This effect is minimised when using the spirit based inks.

Screen printing: a detailed assessment

Transfer papers are produced commercially by a number of different print processes, which have their origins either in the printing of fabrics, or in the printing of paper for packaging, etc.

On a small scale, with equipment which can be easily obtained in most schools, a convenient method of creating paper originals, is to use a flat screen. Although the technique of screen preparation is well known, to produce a successful paper design by this means requires an additional understanding of the basic function of the paper and the versatility of the printing operation.

The paper acts as a supporting material for the finely dispersed particles of dye which are printed on it in the form of a design. Any grade or surface

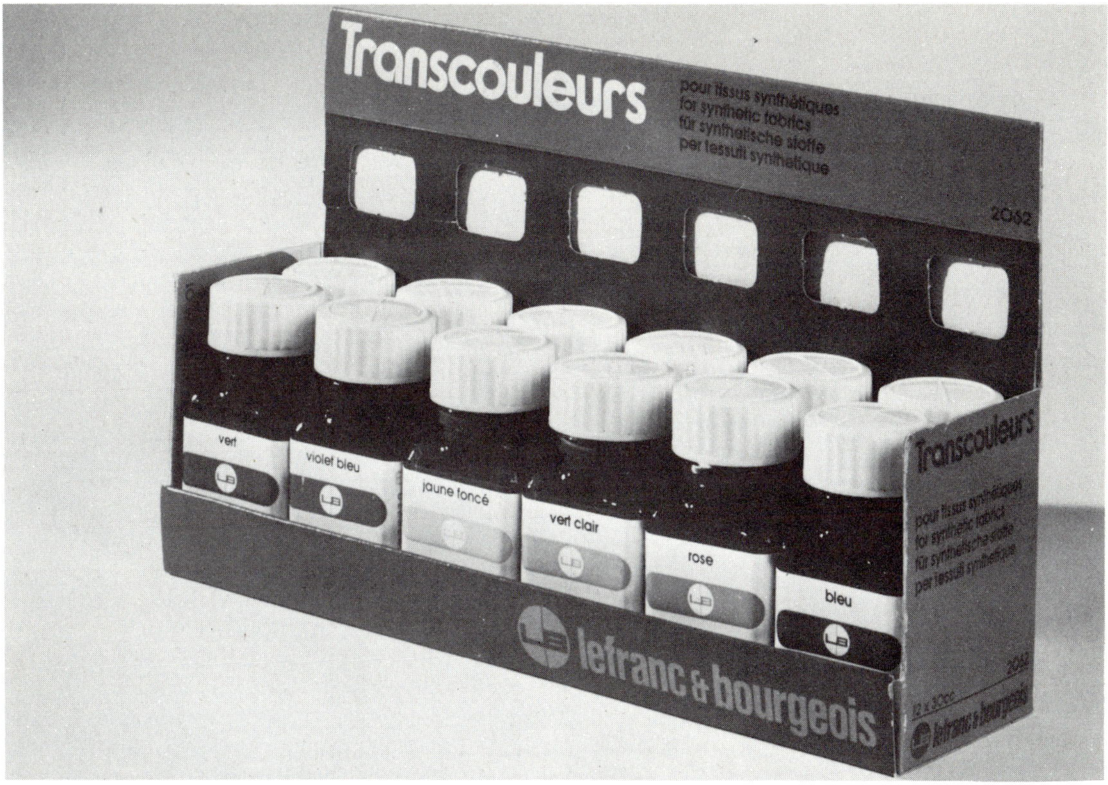

A range of twelve transfer colours in 30 cc jars. Available in individual colours, these inks are ideally suited to the needs of the designer or student who wishes to explore transfer printing for the first time

Examples from the range of transfer inks which are readily available to colleges and schools

structure of paper may be used. However, to achieve the maximum strength of colour transferred onto the fabric it is necessary to deposit the dye particles upon the surface of the paper and so minimise the extent to which they are absorbed into the paper. This may be conveniently carried out by using a highly glazed paper of the 'MG' series. Having made this choice one is faced with the characteristic feature of screen printing which is the deposition of a heavy layer of colour; for if a too heavy a layer of ink is placed upon the paper surface, there inevitably arises the problems concerned with smudging and lack of definition of the image. Various steps may however be taken to minimise this problem.

1 Amend the consistency of the colour paste to be as thick as possible.
2 Use a finer mesh of screen.
3 Use the squeegee in an upright manner and create a hard sharp edge to the blade.
4 Print with the paper lying on a hard surface.

It is by no means uncommon to find that a combination of alterations in technique are necessary and such alterations should be carried out one at a time, to avoid confusion and to allow the student the chance to correctly evaluate the significance of each step.

During this initial period of working there is great value in keeping the printing conditions constant, eg same screen, colour and squeegee and then printing on a variety of papers. A suitable test screen for this work would have a collection of engraved images such as fine lines, small graded spots, fine and coarse textures and larger solid areas.

Having decided that one or two grades of paper are adequate for the type of designs required, one now has the opportunity to try different variations of printing technique to judge whether further improvements can be made.

Overprinting colours

A final point concerning the production of the papers is related to the use of overprinting, ie colours that lay upon each other to give mixtures of shade and chroma. This is an accepted practise in orthodox textile printing and the general rule is that, given two colours of equal strength, the colour that lays upon the fabric first dominates the resulting overprint mixture. For example, if one prints a blue and then overprints a yellow the resultant mixture is a green, but a blue green since the blue dominates.

Overprinting techniques on paper should be carried out with considerable caution as the base material, unlike fabric, is capable of limited absorption. Too much overprinting can yield a too pronounced distortion and cockling of the paper as discussed earlier. In addition the overprint colour affect is the reverse of that previously described on fabric.

If blue is printed on paper and yellow printed over the blue, on the paper, there is a blue dominated green. However when the paper is applied to the fabric, in the transferring operation, the yellow being the last on the paper is the first on the fabric so there is formed a yellow dominated green on the fabric.

As one can appreciate it is therefore essential to carry out carefully small scale trials using overprinting techniques, since it is not uncommon for the colour lying on top of another colour to block its passage completely in the transfer operation. In this extreme a yellow printed over a blue on paper may only give a dull yellow on the fabric rather than a strong green.

Opposite A student at Leicester Polytechnic engaged on a transfer printing project

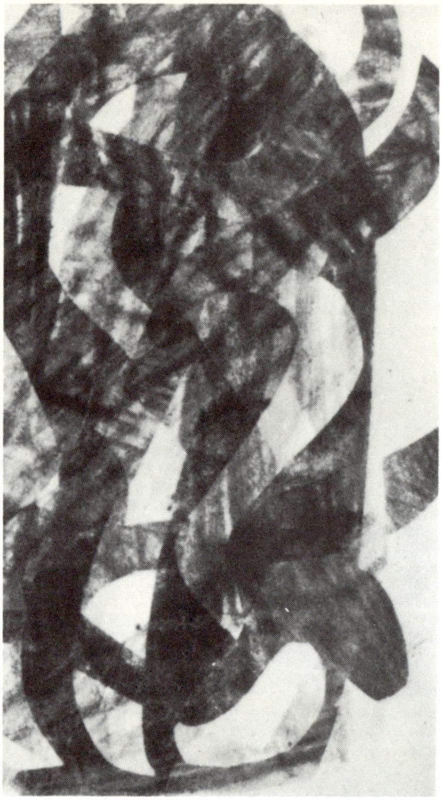

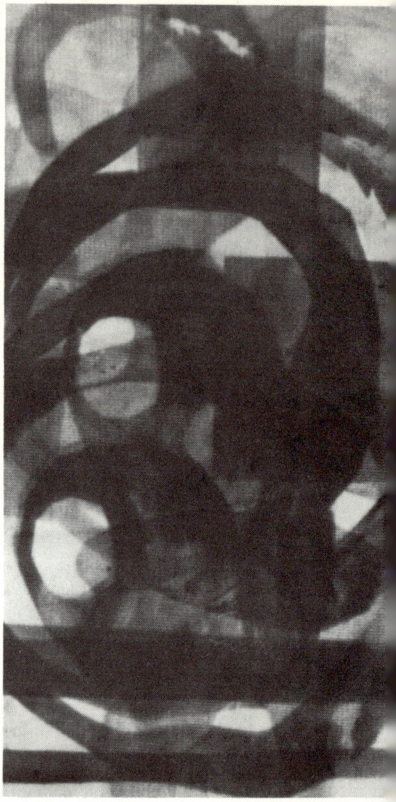

A series of experimental designs printed onto Crimplene using both the transfer crayons and transfer inks. As can be seen in the two examples, *above left*, strips of texture and rubbings using the transfer crayons have been overprinted to create the design whereas in example on *far right* the inks have been used in the same way

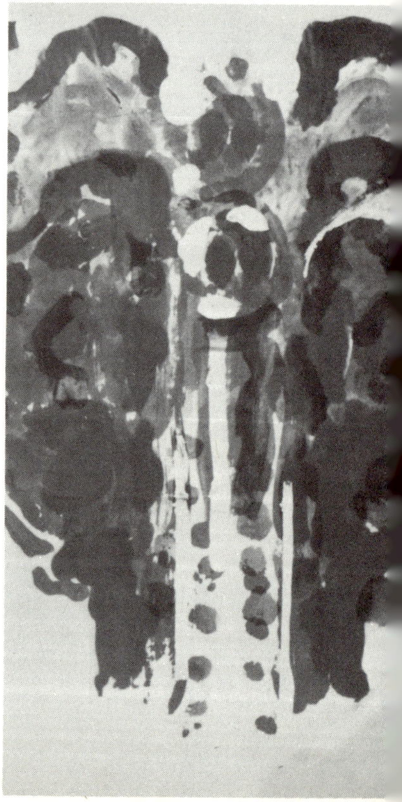

The illustrations right show the different effects which can be achieved using first the crayons and then the inks in isolation

Transfer dyes are applied to paper with a paint brush; the brush marks are explored and the paint surface distorted by running implements across the paper to remove areas of dye; sharp edged shapes are produced by cutting up other paper prints and superimposing them on top of the final paper pattern before transfer

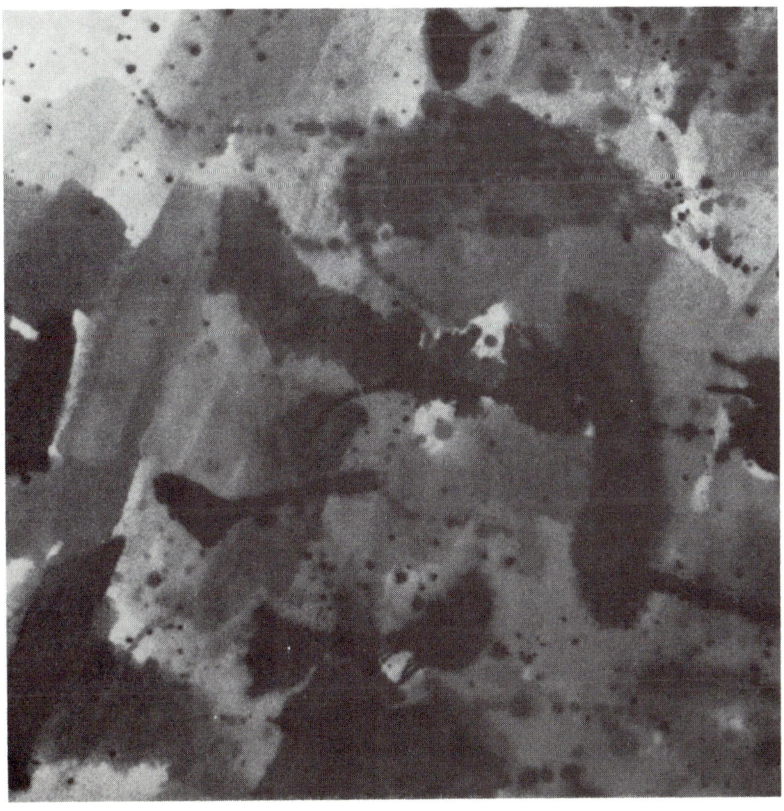

Transfer inks applied to the paper by brush, sponge, splatter technique and blotting, before being finally transferred on to the fabric

Three collage designs incorporating sheets of experimental textures. In the example, *below right*, liquitex acrylic colours have also been added for emphasis. Work from Art Teachers Course, The Hill Residential College, Abergavenny

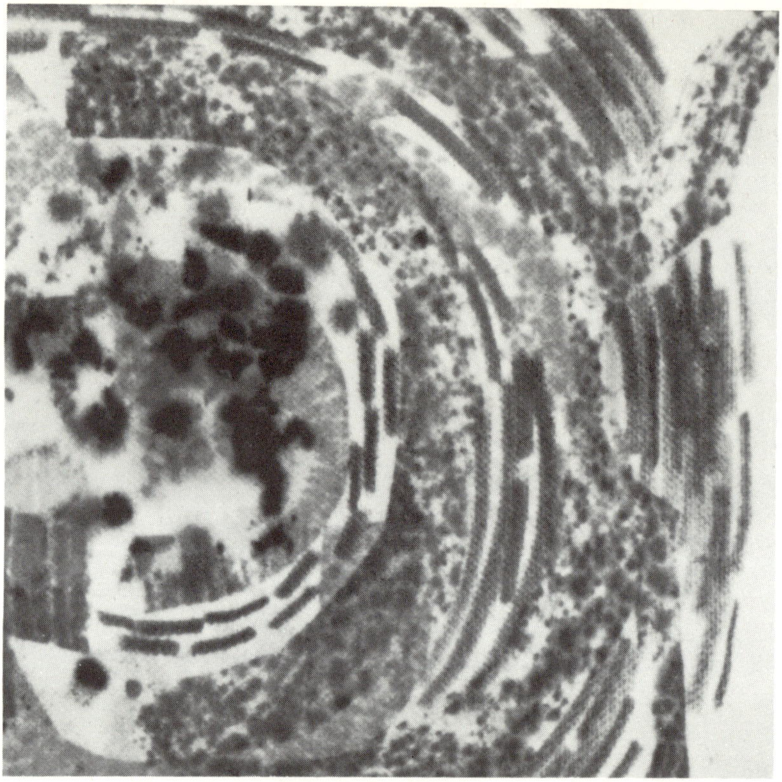

A painting in mixed media which developed from the study below

An analytical study of transfer printing technique. In all these examples a bone form was used as the starting point and every print and paper design was kept for assessment

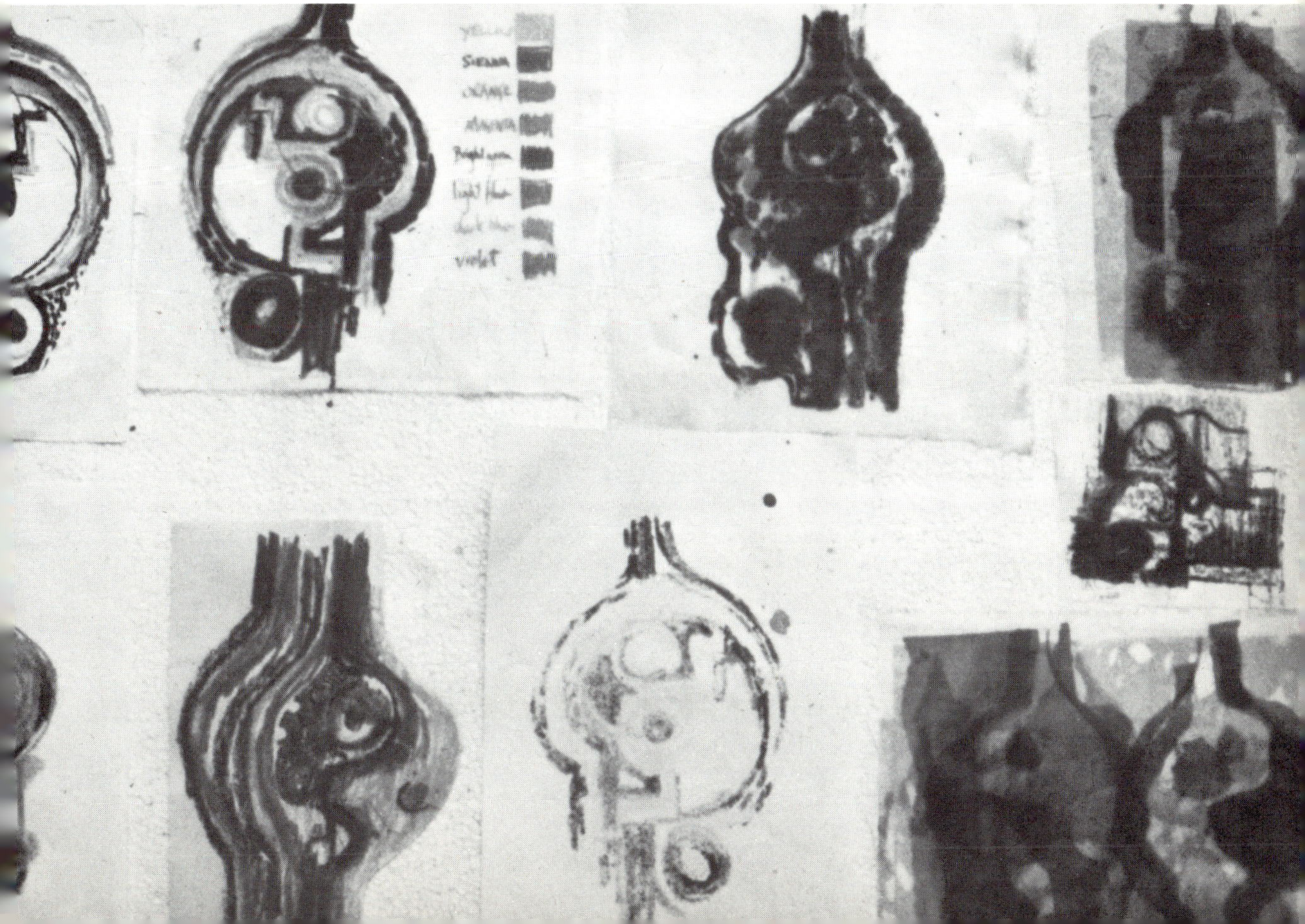

Experimental paintings developed from basic transfer printing exercises. In all these pictures the initial transfer prints were cut up and glued to the prepared background and then used as the starting point for a series of paintings measuring 60 cm × 90 cm (3 ft × 2 ft). The high relief modelling used on some of these pictures is produced by using Liquitex Modelling Paste mixed with Gel Medium. All these examples were produced on a three day course on Acrylics run by the author at The Hill Residential College, Abergavenny

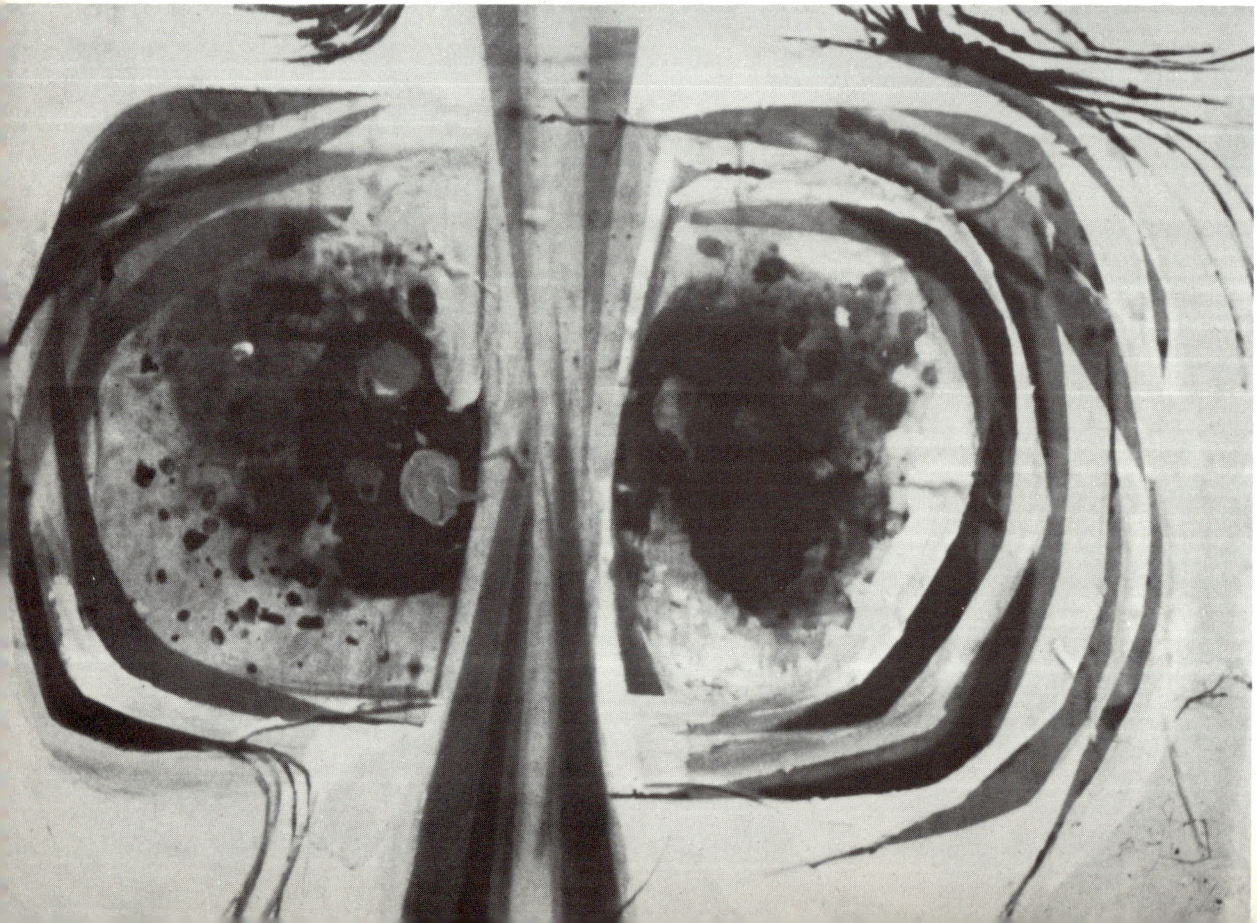

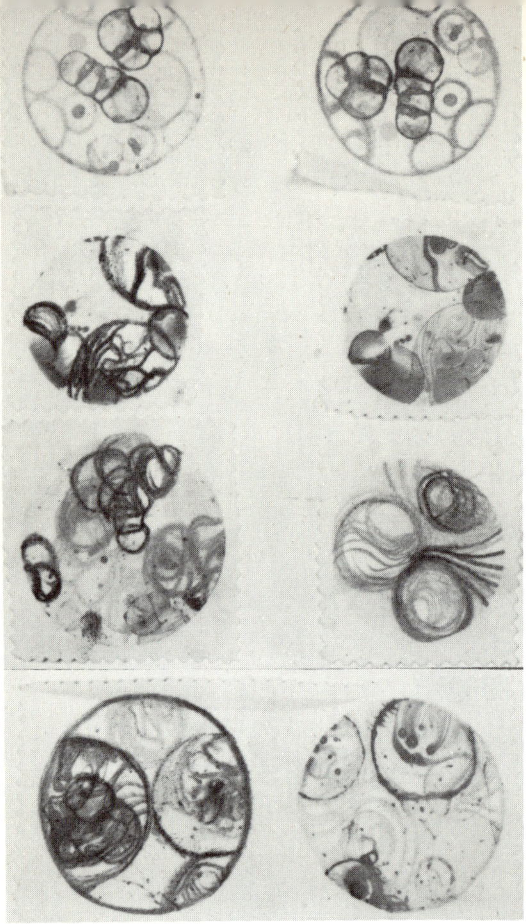

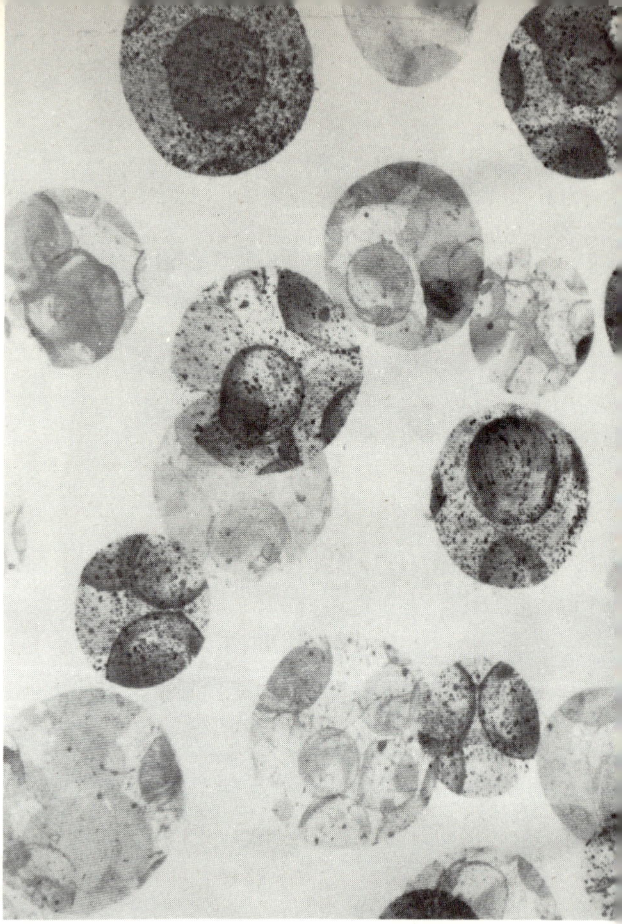

A series of experiments completed by Jane Gabrielle Scott before she produced her *Bubbles* designs. The child's dress which was eventually made up from this fabric is also shown on page 73

Above right *Bubbles* by Jane Gabrielle Scott. To achieve this unique effect the artist mixed liquid detergent with the inks and then blew the bubbles onto paper using an ordinary drinking straw. Each bubble was then cut out and printed individually

A 'tachist' design using the transfer inks in a free way onto paper before transferring the resulting design onto fabric

Bubbles and *Child's Play*, two children's garments by Jane Gabrielle Scott

Patchwork and *Cats*, two children's dresses by Jane Gabrielle Scott

Detail of *Patchwork* dress. To achieve this patchwork effect the designer first produced a wide variety of different colour sheets and textures, which were then cut up and mounted before finally printing the fabric. In some areas overprinting has also been used

Detail of 'Cats' dress. In this design free drawing and resist effects have also been included, together with a range of collage techniques

A selection of transfer printed ties using both transfer crayons and transfer inks to achieve the various effects

A black and white op art design used as the starting point for the distorted textured design right

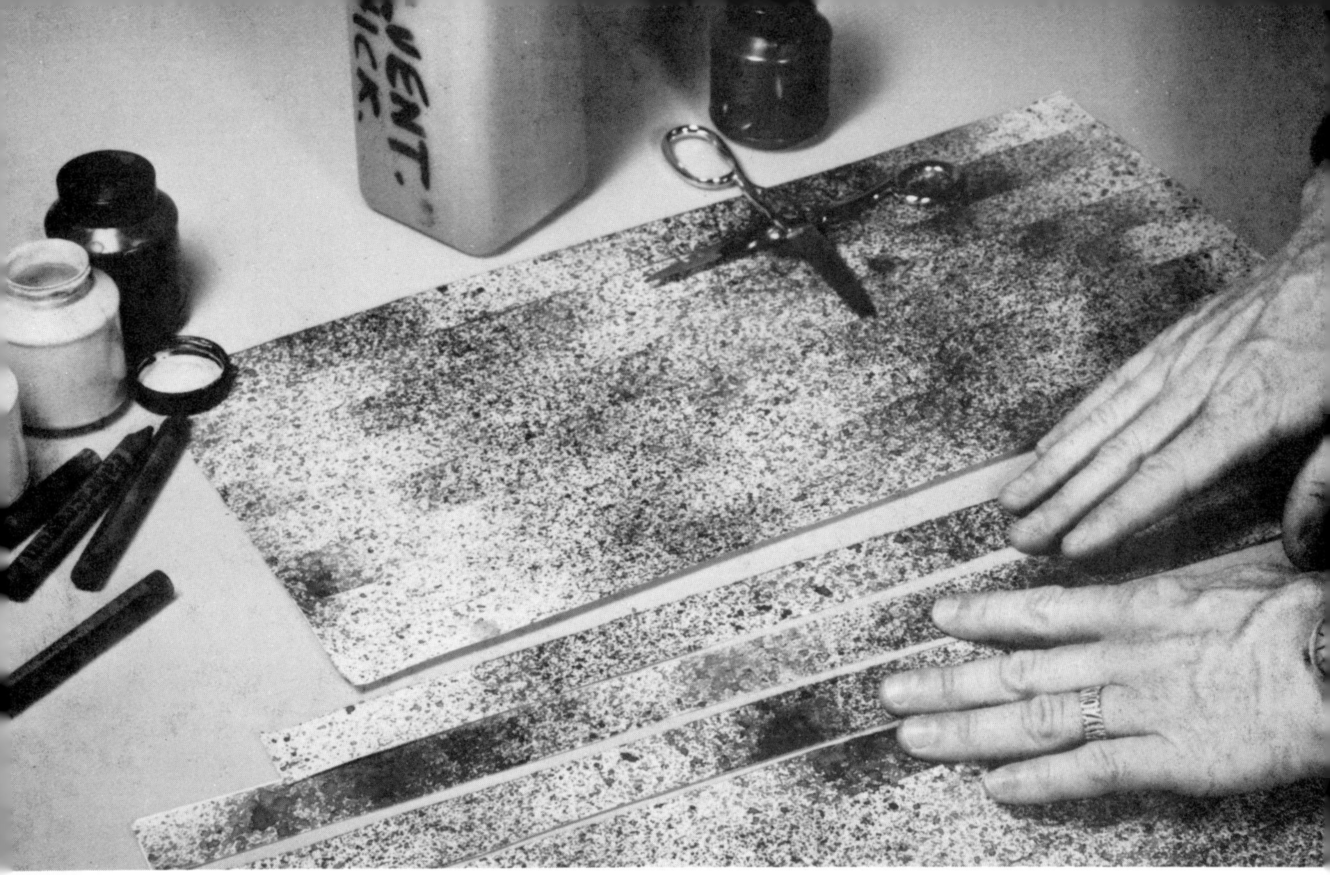

To achieve this effect a large sheet of paper was sprayed with different colours and then cut into strips before being rearranged and mounted onto a backing paper

Although much of the original design is lost when printed, the different coloured strips still vibrate in an optical design

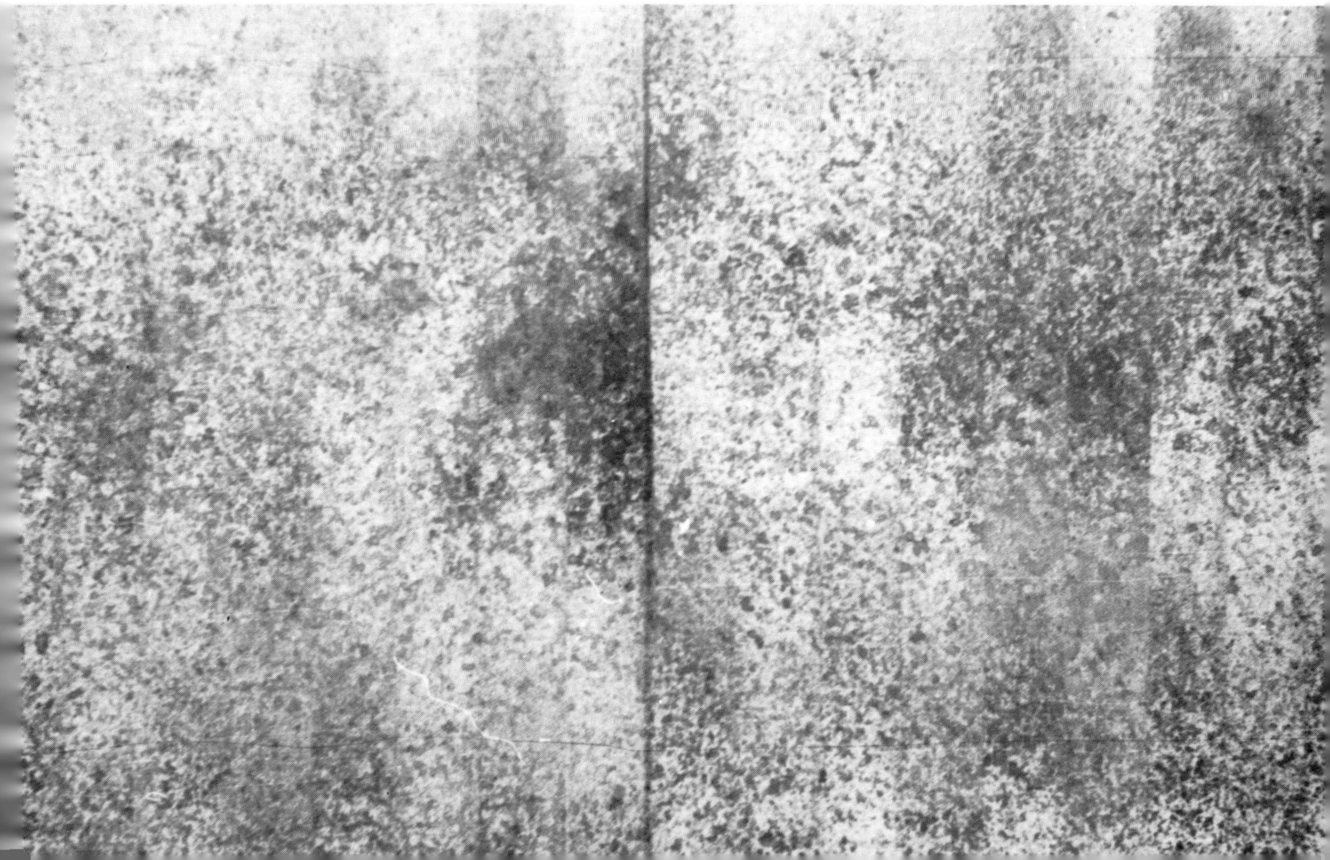

These four sheets of experiments illustrate the enormous variety of different effects which can be achieved using the transfer inks. Sheet 1 shows the effects which can be produced when aqueous inks are diluted with water. Sheet 2 explores the potential of using the algenate thickener to create areas of white within the design before transferring the image onto fabric. Sheet 3 develops the idea of using different fabrics to achieve a variety of effects from the same basic design. Sheet 4 uses a similar technique to sheet 1, but uses white spirit to dilute the spirit based inks to create the same marbling effects

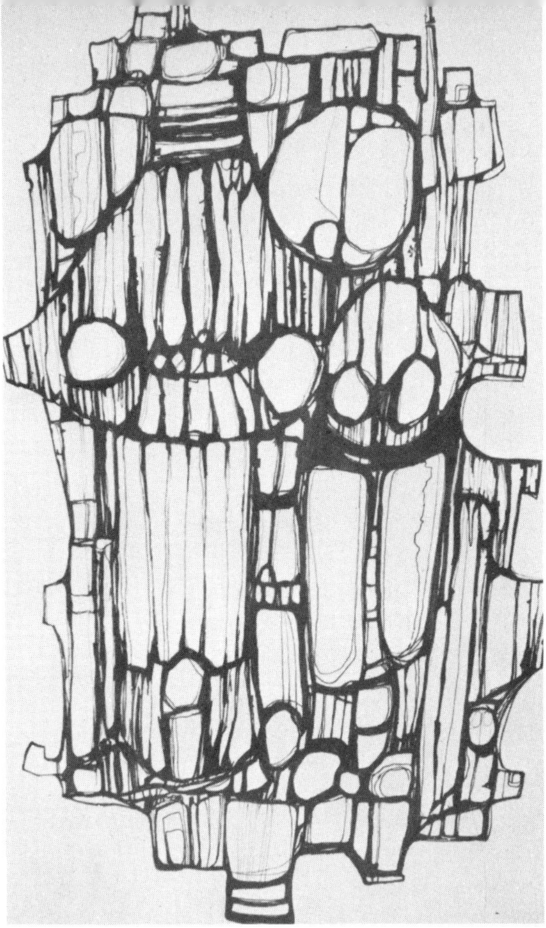

A wall design by the author
Pen and ink

Using the crayons and the inks plus the medium, the author is able to produce exactly the type of textural effects he requires

A detailed drawing of an agate stone which was used as the starting point for a series of transfer printed designs

A development of the agate theme. A free interpretation of the original design is cut up and transferred onto a variety of tinted fabrics. The design thus retains a unity of colour and the painted areas are used as a contrast to the flat unprinted negative shapes

The agate design using resist techniques and diluted areas of colour to achieve a marbled effect

A paper collage using tissue paper, thread, chalk, and pieces of transfer paper. As the design is still retained on the paper after being transferred the designer is given the opportunity of creating many different end results as the project progresses

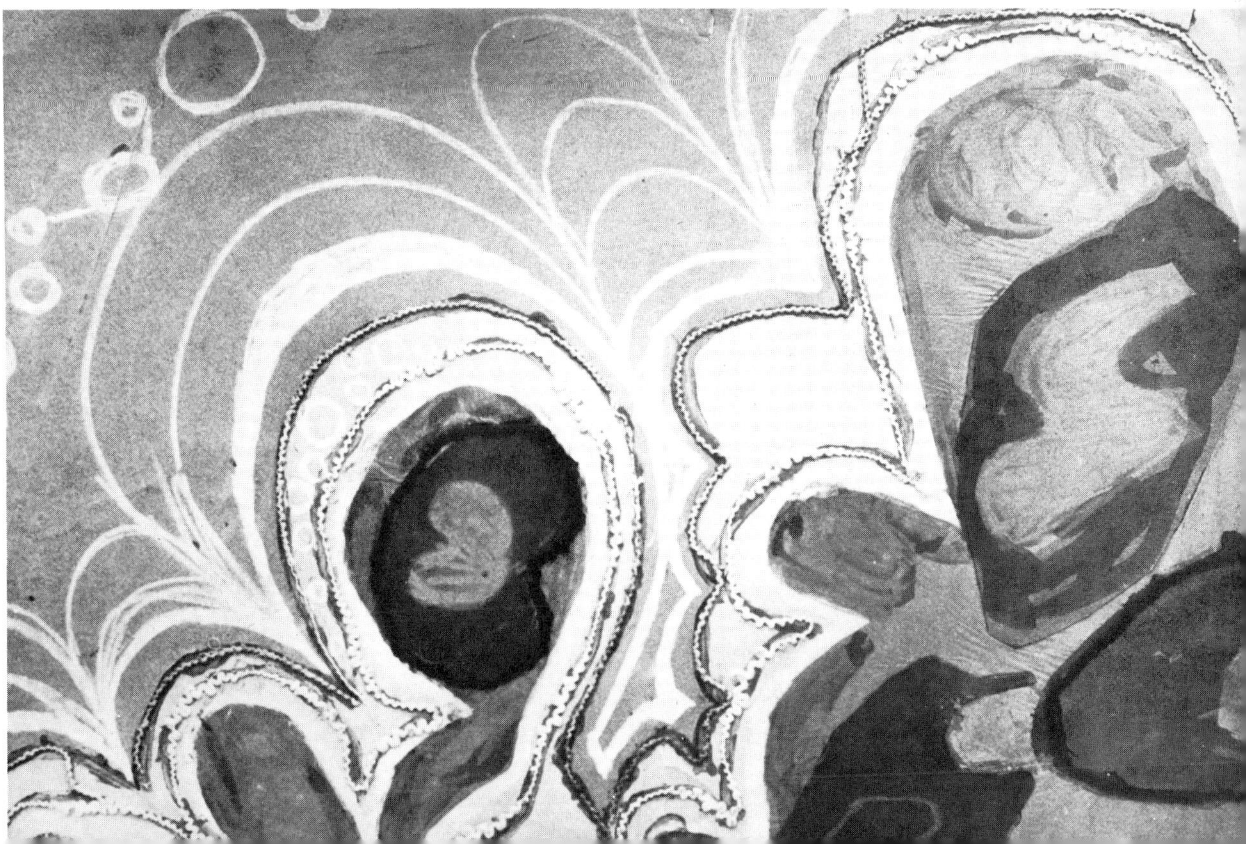

A high quality drawing which was translated into a transfer print

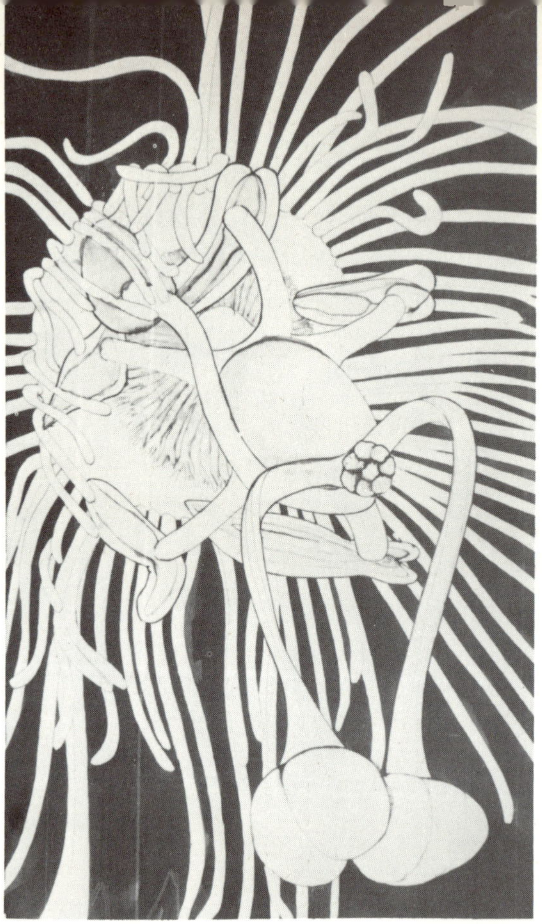

Two 'flow' designs created specifically for transfer printing; both designs to be screen printed

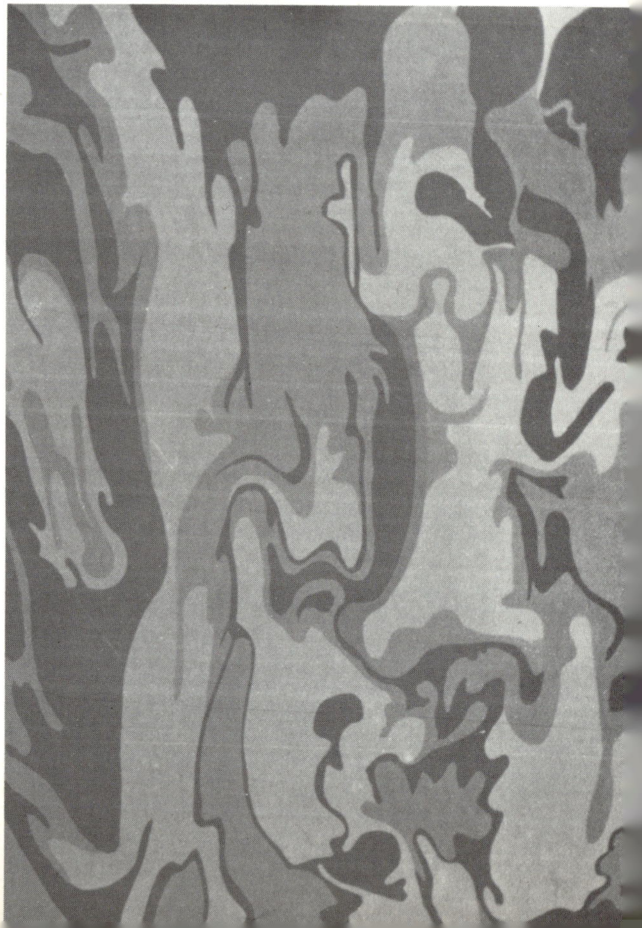

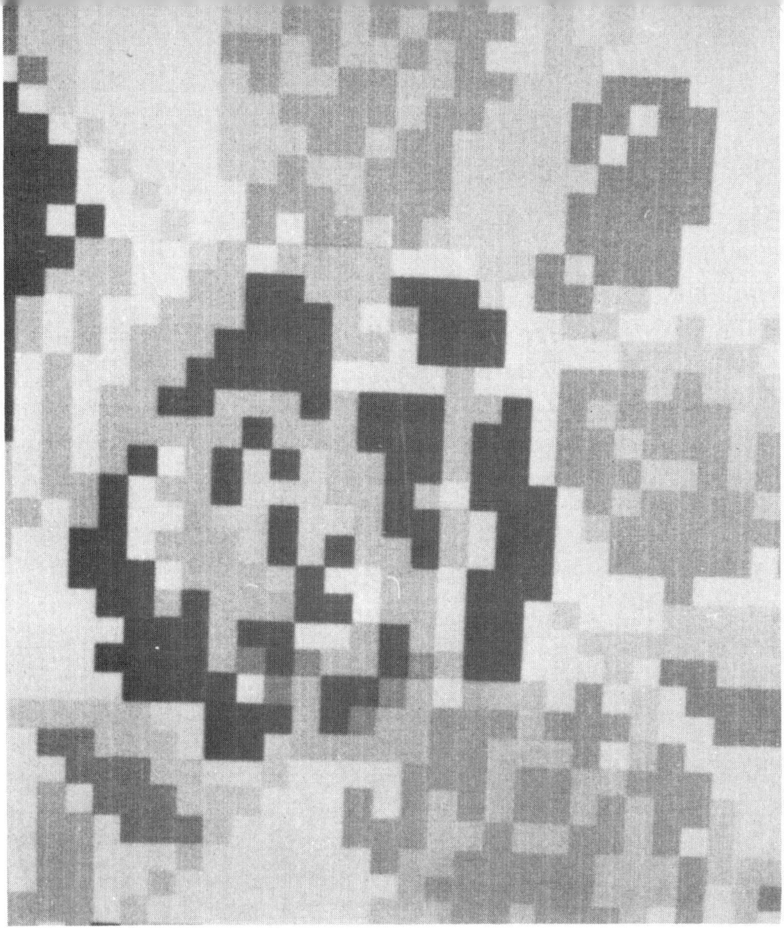

A four colour screen printed design used as a furnishing fabric. Although the paper was printed in four stages, the final design onto the fabric was completed in one operation, with a high degree of accuracy

A series of hand painted leaf forms using transfer inks, by Leicester Polytechnic Department of Printed Textiles

A number of different 'colour ways' of the same design which have been screen printed and then transfer printed to see which was the most successful, by Leicester Polytechnic

A complex design created from an organic form and then transfer printed, by Leicester Polytechnic student

A repeated design created by printing the same paper original a number of times. This technique is particularly successful if a transfer press is used

A decorative patchwork design which incorporates a great variety of different transfer printed effects. This has been sewn together from individual squares, whereas the children's patchwork was produced onto one paper original in a collage technique

6 Transfer printing as a craft activity

In all the work considered so far the students have been encouraged to experiment freely with the end results being used as collages, decorative panels, and even as starting points for paintings. However as the students grow more technically expert a more objective approach can be adopted and the transfer printed designs used for more utilitarian objects, from shoe bags to high fashion, and it is this type of work which will be looked at in this chapter.

The most obvious advantage, in terms of designs, that transfer printing offers is that the drawn image can be transferred onto the fabric very quickly. Whereas in most of the traditional methods of textile printing many weeks are taken in preparation before the final design can be assessed on the fabric. This does not mean, however, that the process is superficial and just as much thought should be given to the quality of the design, fabric selection and fabric utilisation as with conventional screen or block printing. For I have found that many students mistake the ease of actually putting the design onto the fabric, with a need to rush the design side of the work and consequently only produce very limited results.

One therefore sees the need at this stage of developing a very professional attitude to both the designing and transfer of the fabric, for as emphasised before, the process is very simple although all stages of printing must be carried out very carefully and accurately if the results are to be of the required standard. As this process has the unique characteristic of being a dry print process onto the fabric I can see many advantages of completing the actual printing in the dress area of a design department and so creating a positive link between the creation of the design and its utilisation.

Another area of work relating to transfer printing generally, which also creates this link between design and home economics, is the study of colour fastness and light fastness in terms of synthetic fabrics.

If this project is to be considered one first has to obtain a variety of different fabrics which are then cut into long strips, approximately four inches wide. These strips are then transfer printed with horizontal stripes of colour and cut vertically into two. This produces two identical strips so that one piece can be washed and the other used as a control (to see how much colour has been lost after washing). Different temperatures of washing can be included in these tests, as can different detergents.

The results are quite fascinating and often unexpected, especially if mixtures and coated fabrics of all types are included.

In the same study light fastness could also be considered, again using a control which would be kept in a sealed box. Here the results would be much slower, although very obvious, even when using a simple window sill test. Ultra violet and infra red lights would also give interesting results and here again the Science Department could be involved.

NOTE Manufacturers have their own scale of quality acceptance in both these areas and a study of these gradings would also prove of interest as can be seen in the illustration a great variety of end results can be completed from simple household items to sophisticated dress designs and a wide selection of fabrics can also be successfully printed. Obviously the industrial process allows all over patterns to be produced which look exactly like conventional screen prints. I feel however that the main strength of this process in schools and home dressmaking is not to copy industrial techniques but to use transfer printing to enrich and personalize areas of a garment. As we can see in many of the examples this method of working is most successful if the original motif on paper is very carefully cut out before transfer.

In the same way if one wishes to decorate a cotton garment, or apply a detailed design onto a very dark background, this can easily be achieved simply by cutting out, not only the paper design, but also the final print which can then be sewn onto the base fabric. This technique is particularly successful if individual emblems or pockets are being considered, and the recent fashion for decorating duffle bags could also be exploited in this way.

At the same level of working, some exciting work can be achieved by students who wish to draw up-to-date pop symbols and then transfer these onto their old white nylon shirts or specially made sweaters or tank tops. I can see no reason why this type of work is not just as relevant as the more conventional design forms, as long as the symbols or letters are carefully considered and accurately transferred.

In the more traditional dressmaking field, one sees possibly the most potential for transfer printing, as dresses, blouses, skirts, ties, children's clothes, etc, can all be enriched either before or after they have been made up. For example several different colour-ways could be printed for the cuffs and collar on a dress before the final choice is made. In the same way a quite unique garment can be created from the simplest of the mass produced paper patterns. As so many of these paper patterns have been designed specifically for synthetic fabrics the dressmaker is often looking for a way to personalise their garments and therefore not be restricted by the availability of commercial prints.

Finally to return to a more experimental approach, one can see the enormous possibilities of using this print process to create such items as: unusual cushions, unique dolls and toys for children, highly individual dress accessories, and even the ultimate in 'soft sculptures'.

NOTE For professional results it is most important to remember that the smallest speck of crayon will print. It is therefore essential to complete the paper design away from the transfer area. This area should also be clean with the top sheet of the transfer bed renewed before each print.

If a design is to be printed on a tee-shirt or blouse, newspaper or a number of sheets of plain paper should be placed between the front and back of the garment so that the printed image does not ghost through.

A decorative design transferred onto a crimplene scarf using *Finart Fabricrayon*

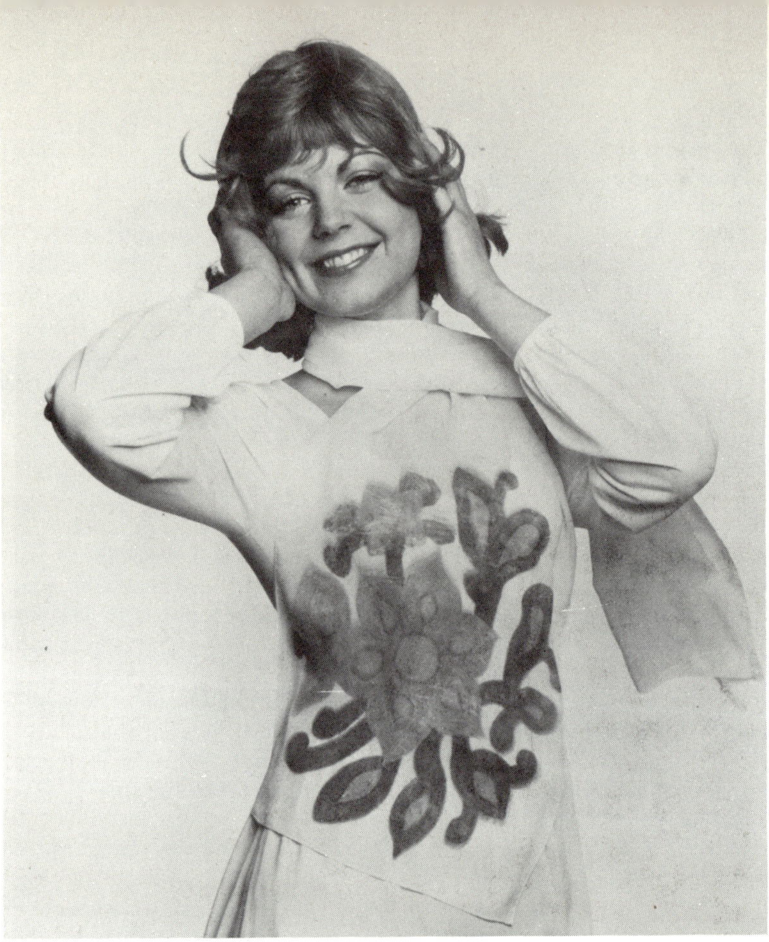

A zodiac sign used as the motif on a scarf accessory in a similar technique to previous design. In all this type of work it is essential for the original design to be cut out very carefully

A design produced in line and texture; the textural areas are produced from rubbings taken from a Victorian tile

A rubbing from a string block using transfer crayons. By adopting this technique the artist is able to create multiples from the same original design and then print them as border prints

A decorative symmetrical design to be printed onto a cushion with transfer crayons

A stylised flower design produced for the commercial tee-shirt market (screen printed)

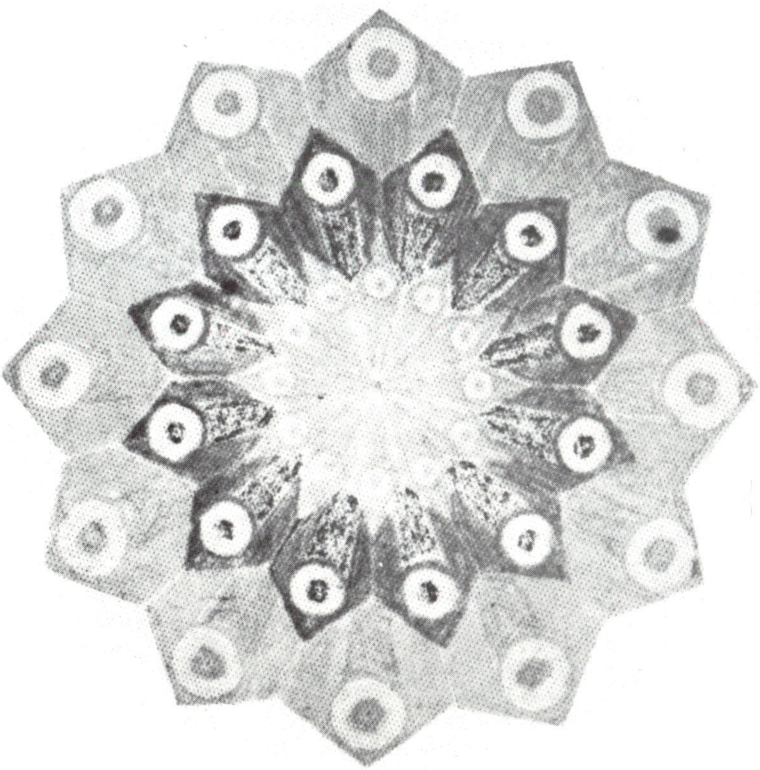

A detailed symmetrical design created in transfer crayons. Design by Frank Birtwhistle

Batman and Rupert Bear characters drawn in Finart Fabricrayons and used to decorate children's tee-shirts, shoe-bags, etc. This technique is ideal for personalising this type of item. In all cases the designs are cut out before transfer

A series of designs using transfer crayons printed and applied to a wide variety of garments and accessories. This method of working is particularly successful when the motif is cut out and applied onto a dark background, which can be made of either synthetic or natural fabric. Designs from The Studio, Binney and Smith, New York

Art Deco designs used as original pockets for children's play smocks

This photograph shows the enormous flexibility of this technique in terms of enriching household items such as cushions, tea-towels, hats and school-bags. Designs from The Studio, Binney and Smith, New York

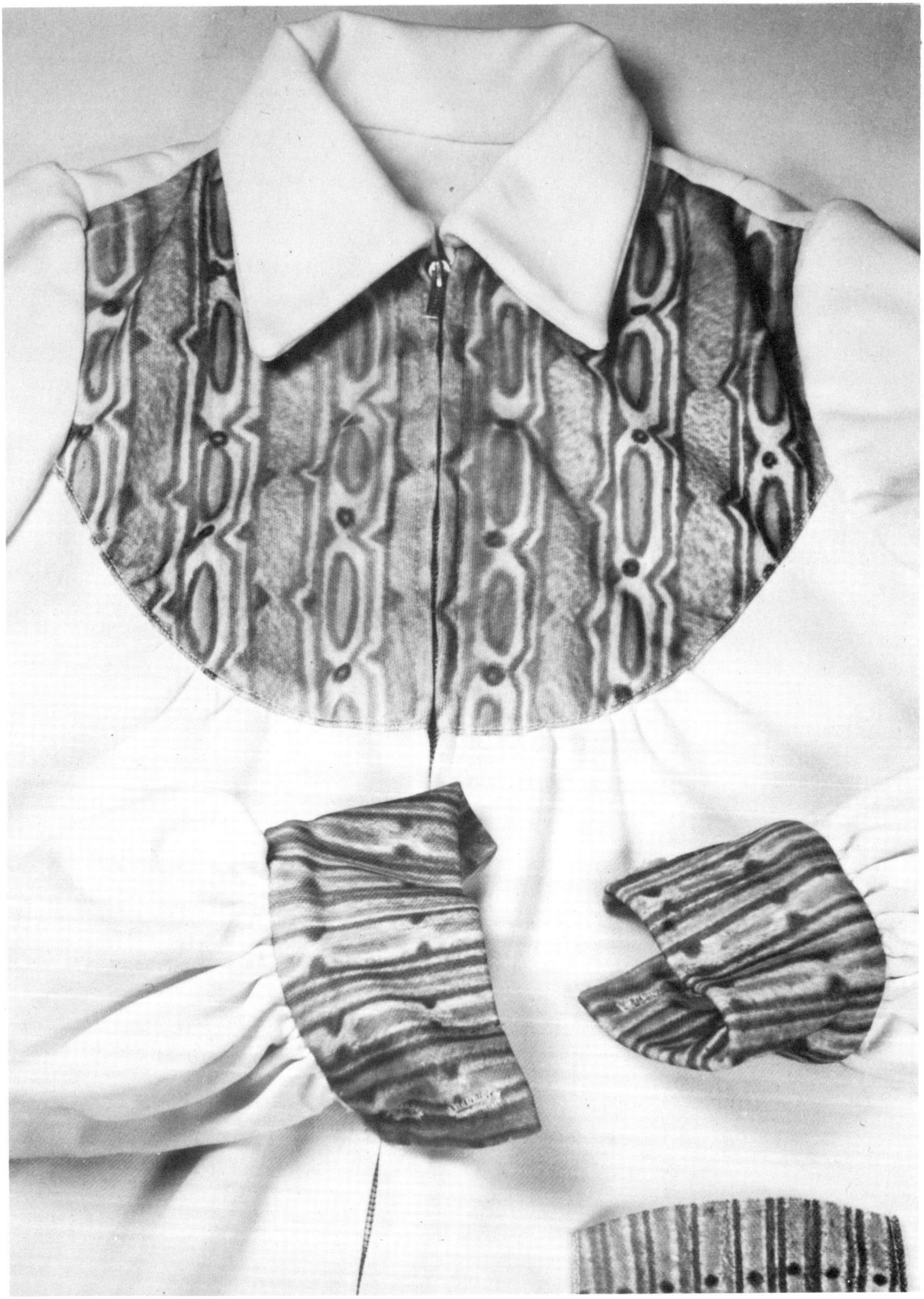

A sophisticated Mexican motif transferred as a single panel onto a white sundress

Left A sophisticated teenage party dress which incorporates panels of transfer printing. By using this method of working the designer can produce a number of different design panels before making the final choice. Design by Frank Birtwhistle, dress created by Margaret Birtwhistle

Colour plate facing courtesy of Transprint (UK) Limited

One of the original designs for the BBC programme *Tomorrow's World*. Design by the author

Colour plate facing
Courtesy of Transprint (UK) Limited

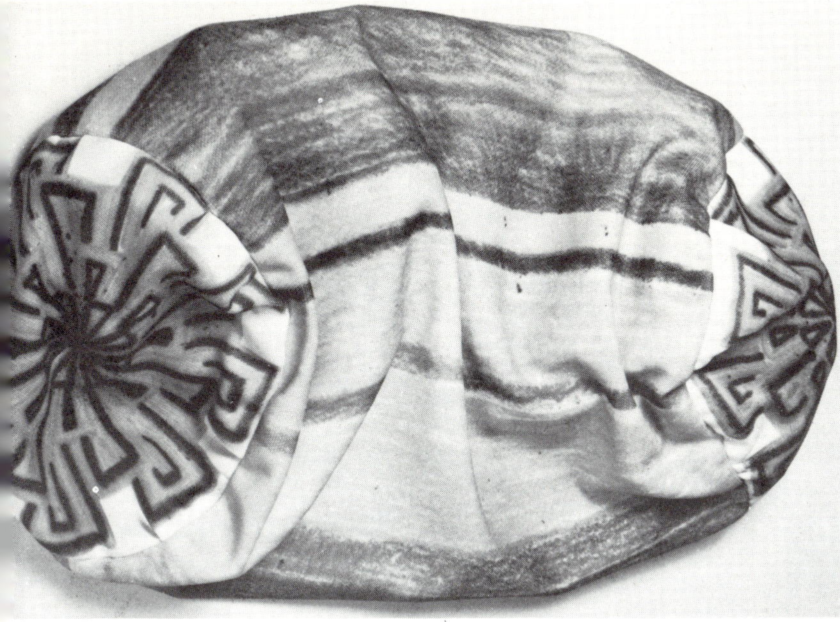

A three-section pyjama case with each panel transfer printed before being made up

Below and overleaf A design project using Bordina paper fabric to create a series of dresses which were made up and worn by the students themselves. Some of the decoration was printed directly onto the fabric and others were applied as decorative motifs. Sixth Form Project, Royal Latin School, Buckingham

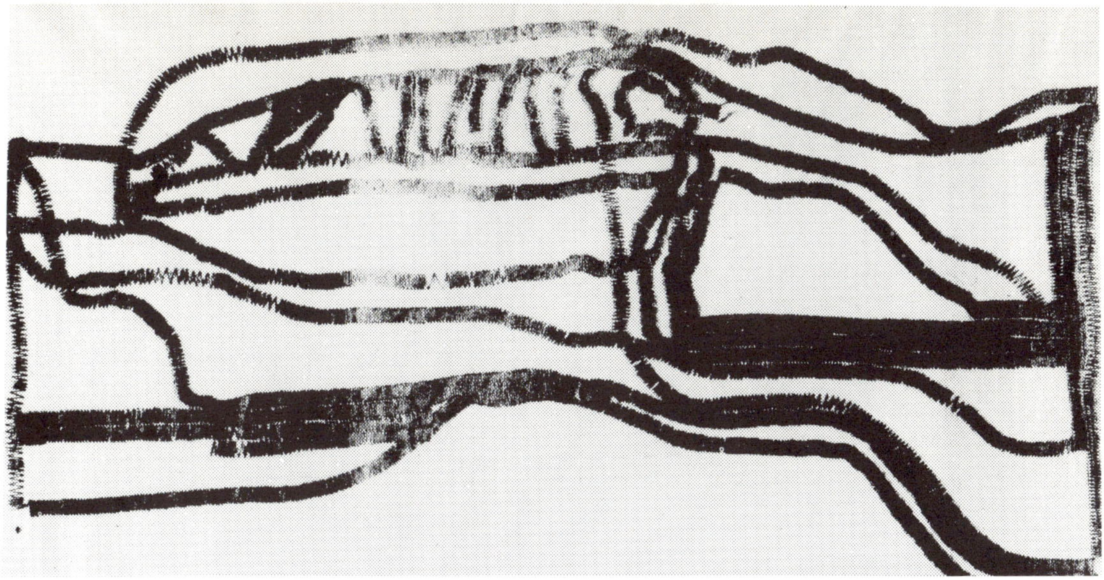

Far right, top Experimental embroidery. Cotton material embroidered with a satin stitch using a synthetic thread. The design was then printed with a serisol dye (for cotton) and transfer crayons, the transfer print only transferring onto the embroidery with the cotton acting as a resist. Design by Sue Mann, Leicester Polytechnic

Wall hanging by Sarah Hobson. In this hanging the various motifs have been transfer printed and then quilted and embroidered to produce the original relief effects

Quilt by Holly Dianne Shaw, New York, produced in Crayola Craft Fabric Crayons (child size, approx. 90 cm × 120 cm (3 ft × 4 ft). The squares of synthetic fabric were first coloured with fabric crayons and then sewn and embroidered to a woven brown cotton corduroy backing. The quilt was then bordered and backed with green corduroy and quilted by hand

A range of dress designs specifically created for transfer printing by a designer who has a comprehensive knowledge of the different effects which can be achieved using this technique

A series of small border prints to be transfer printed onto selected areas of the garment before being made up. The designer logically develops her idea on paper before committing the final design onto fabric

7 A summary of fashion usage

To appreciate fully the potential of transfer printing it is interesting to look at the many different textile groupings and sub-groupings which are now being printed by this process. I have therefore listed below the various ways in which heat transfer papers are now being used commercially. As mentioned in the introduction one can easily see how many of these groupings can be re-applied for use in schools and in turn home dressmaking and further education work.

Fashion fabrics

Women's fashions

Dresses: formal wear, uniforms, housecoats and aprons, maternity wear, bridal gowns, junior wear and junior petite misses in knitted and woven fabrics

Lingerie: robes and nightwear, slips and foundation garments such as bras, tights and girdles

Coats: casuals, raincoats, fun furs (imitation fur types), *Vinel*, *Teklan* and *Dylan*

Sportswear: woven and knitted pants, sweaters, skirts, co-ordinates, tops and bathing costumes

Men's wear

Clothing: suits, sports coats, slacks, raincoats, topcoats, accessories such as shirts, ties, pyjamas, robes, beachwear, knitted and woven sweaters, socks

Children's fashions

dresses and playsuits

Underwear: slips and panties

Sleepwear: pyjamas, gowns and robes which also includes babywear

Shoes: slippers and playshoes

Sportswear: blouses, shirts and skirts

Bathing and beachwear

Home furnishings

Furniture: suite coverings, unupholstered stretched covers, deckchair and outdoor chair coverings, moulded furniture

Bedding: mattress and box covers, sheets and duvets

Curtains and draperies: including curtains, net curtains, blinds and shades, towelling and shower curtains

Rugs and carpeting: these include needle felts, stitch bonded, low pile needle, flock (3-mm/$\frac{1}{8}$ in.) woven cord, scatter rugs, toilet sets and warp yarns

Dish towels: printed with tourist motifs

Lampshade fabrics

Dinner ware: place settings, tablecloths and even bar mats

Wallcoverings: using laminated hessian and warp thread effects.

In addition one has seen a recent development in the use of mod-acrylic fibres which do not support combustion and are therefore fire resistant, and so are used for blankets and in particular electric blankets.

Left A twenties design used to decorate a synthetic tee-shirt. Transfer printing is particularly suitable for this type of single motif decoration

A single motif transfer paper. Note how the paper design has to be printed in reverse so that the lettering is the right way round on the fabric after transfer

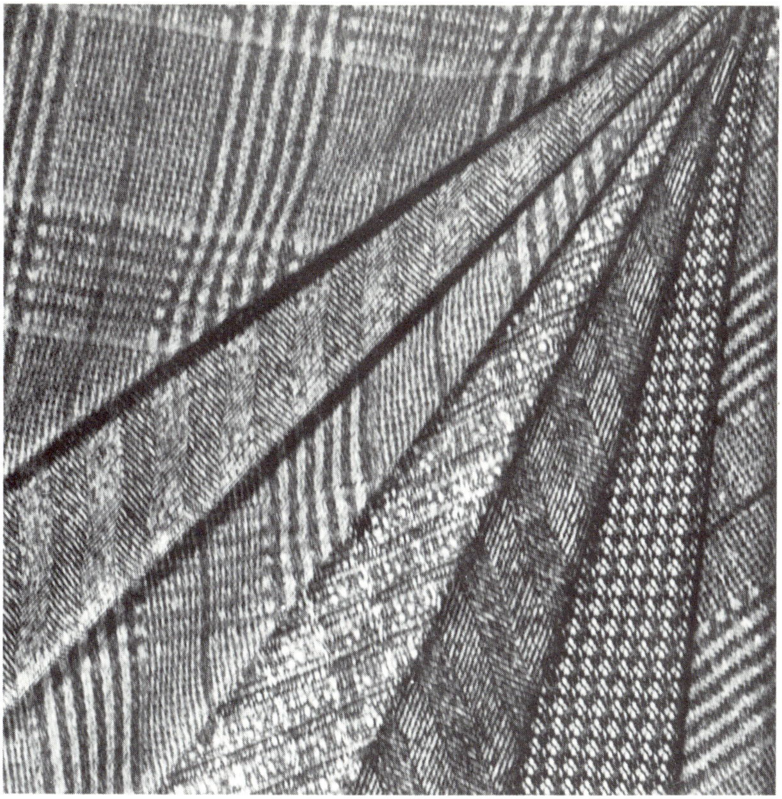

A range of simulated woven designs from the Sublistatic Collection. This method of printing crimplene and trevira is particularly interesting as it allows a traditional look with the advantages of a smooth man-made surface in terms of dry-cleaning, etc.

Opposite A unique method of transfer printing pleated skirts to create a fascinating broken design when the skirt is worn. Design by Sketchleys

Detail of simulated woven designs from the Sublistatic library

Transfer printed day wear
by Sublistatic, Geneva

A large scale paper design
120 cm × 90 cm (4 ft × 3 ft)
created specifically for
printing onto a white nylon
rug, suitable for a children's
room

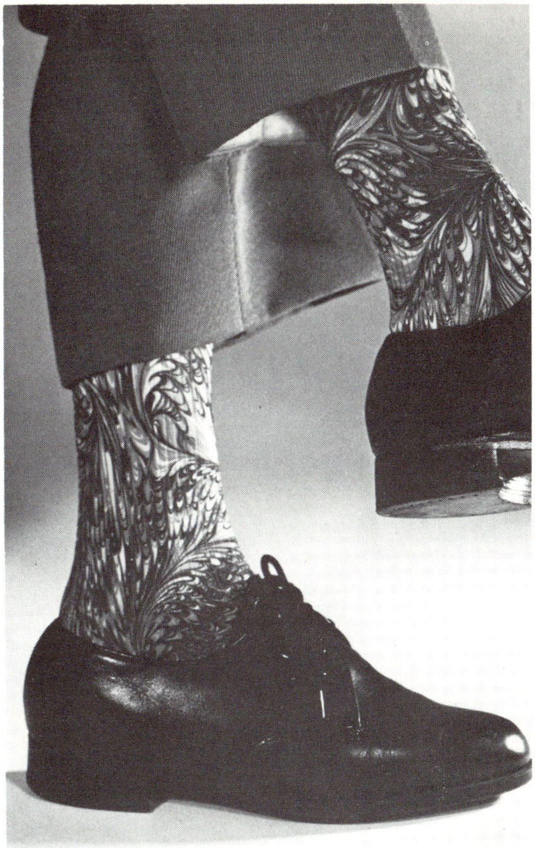

Above left Sublistatic printed half-hose. In this technique the design for the trousers can be easily reproduced on the socks and other accessories such as ties and handkerchiefs

Above right Sublistatic printed half-hose

Flotasia by Flo-Tech Corp, USA. In this commercial technique transfer inks have been used in a similar way to traditional marbling to create the paper original. A piece of fabric and a tie produced from the design are also shown

8 The commercial process

In this chapter and the following we look at the commercial methods of heat transfer printing in more detail. Although the information given is technical it does allow the student to look at examples of transfer printing and begin to appreciate the particular difficulties involved. In addition he also might be able to deduce which print process was used to create the original paper designs. Finally the study of the heat transfer stage, which often uses vast equipment as we can see from the illustration on page 109, gives the student the ideal background to assess the relative merits of the smaller presses which are more suitable for school and college use.

Diagram showing the heat transfer printing route:

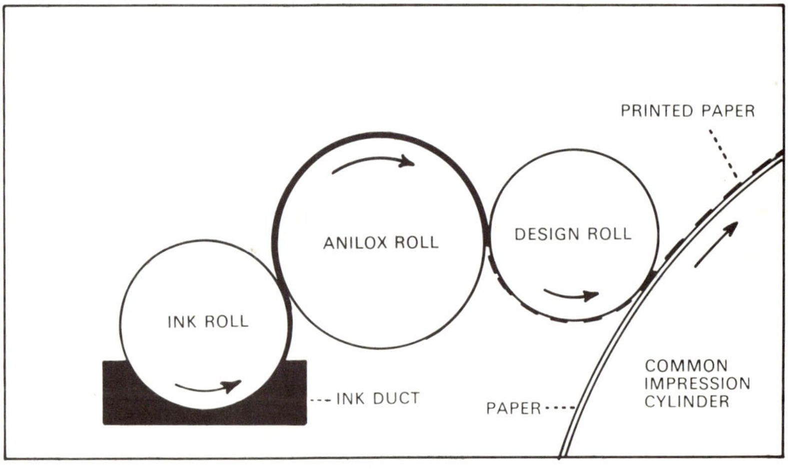

Diagram of how paper is printed by the flexographic method. The ink is picked up from the ink duct by an ink roll, transferred to the anilox roll, from there it goes to the design roll on which are mounted the flexographic printing plates, and from there it is transferred to the paper which is st etched around a common impression cylinder. The whole collection is called a printing unit, and there will be four or six of these units mounted around the common impression cylinder. Courtesy of Strachan and Henslaw Ltd, Bristol

As we can see from this diagram and the summary of transfer printing in the proceeding chapters, this process requires the following five conditions to be met in order to give satisfactory end results, at a commercial level:

1 A carefully selected and prepared fabric.
2 A synthetic fabric having the necessary physical, chemical and thermoplastic properties to withstand the high processing temperature.

3 A range of dispersed dyes which sublime at elevated temperatures, preferably in a narrow temperature band and which have affinity for the synthetic fabric to be printed and little or no affinity for the paper support.
4 A means of printing the paper to meet the high quality of today's textile design market.
5 A method of transferring the design from paper to fabric.

The preparation of the fabric

As one can see in the majority of textile printing techniques the fabrics for transfer printing need to be prepared correctly before printing, if the required colour fastness is to be guaranteed. One must however accept that a large amount of fabric printed in this process is transfer printed without any pre-treatment. These fabrics however would not meet the recognised International Standards for colour fastness.

One therefore sees the importance of adequately desizeing woven fabrics, followed by efficient solvent or aqueous scouring before being printed. For the same reason one sees the importance of 'heat setting' most synthetic fabrics and this should be carried out at a temperature at least equal to and preferably higher than the transferring temperature, otherwise fabric movement can occur during the transfer stage.

Suitable fabrics

As we have discussed earlier the majority of synthetic fabrics are suitable for heat transfer printing including mixtures, providing the proportion of synthetic fibre is in excess of the cellulosic or natural fibre.

In addition to these fabrics many PVC and polyurethane materials can be printed on a variety of surfaces as one can see in chapter 10.

Dyestuffs

The dyes used in transfer printing are chosen from a selection of disperse type dyes which sublime in the region of 180–230°C. These dyes have the added properties of having no affinity for cellulosic based papers which are used as the design support. In addition they are also readily absorbed in their vapour state by most synthetic fibres.

The dyestuffs selected must give adequate depth of shade and colour fastness on the chosen fabric to meet the particular needs of the end usage. In turn the dyes chosen must sublime at a similar rate of vaporisation when used in mixtures, especially when used for blacks, dark greens and browns.

In more technical terms the most suitable dyes seem to be those with a molecular weight of between 240 and 340. The main consideration being that dyes with a lower molecular weight are most suitable for acetates, whereas the higher molecular weights produce higher colour fastness on polyamides.

Ink preparation

Traditionally the inkmaker has produced an ink that was permanent when printed onto paper. The formulation of heat transfer inks obviously requires different criteria. For a transfer ink needs to be formulated to not only meet the special requirements of the paper print process chosen, but also needs to be completely suitable for the subsequent transfer operation in terms of quality of print and end use.

One therefore sees the formulation of the ink being made up as follows:

(a) Disperse dyes. Selected as described above.

(b) Media. Based on water, ethanol, ethylene glycol or toluene.

(c) Resins. These are needed to bind the dye to the paper thus ensuring accuracy of print, and yet they should not hinder the vaporization of the dye by dye-resin interaction or by thermoplastic interaction of the dye and the binder to the fibre. Alkylcelluloses and in particular ethylcellulose are very suitable as they aid the release of the dye vapour during transfer.

(d) Thickeners and other additives. The viscosity of the ink can be altered to suit the printing process and thickeners such as gilsonite and silica can be used. Other agents can be added to loosen the internal structure of the polymer and thus aid fibre penetration.

NOTE In many art schools the water soluble thickener, algenate, is widely used as a thickening agent, in conjunction with the range of disperse dyes which are available in concentrated form. However any soluble thickener could be used such as water paste, starch and even liquid detergent and some exciting results can be achieved if the student is prepared to experiment.

Paper selection

Any material that has no substantivity for disperse dyes can be used as the substrate for transfer printing, but paper is obviously chosen because of its low cost. In this area two types of transfer printed paper are used:

1 Papers that have an adhesive present to avoid slippage during the printing of poorly set fabrics and in sheet form printing on fully fashioned garments.

Heliogravure printing press in a French factory at Taucering Sublistatic

2 Papers containing no adhesive and thus used on temperature sensitive fabrics, eg acrylics, where the speed of sublimation is essential and where a tack adhesive would inhibit the transfer.

Air-knife or blade-coated papers are suitable for gravure, machine glazed kraft papers for flexography and bonded and cartridge paper for letterpress and lithography. In all cases the paper surface should be smooth and non-fibrous and the paper should contain no heavy metals which could act selectively on the dyes.

About 10–3% of the original dye remains on the paper after use and in certain cases these papers can be re-used, ie for lingerie. However for top quality fashion garments this process is not recommended.

The printing of the paper design

The printing of the transfer papers can be carried out by all of the methods widely used in the paper and packaging industry. These techniques can be listed as follows: gravure, flexographic, lithographic, letterpress, rotary screen, flat screen.

A brief description of these various paper printing techniques is given below:

Gravure (maximum paper width (2·1 m/84 in.), maximum number of colours 6)

By far the largest proportion of transfer papers available today are printed by this technique. For this method gives by far the best design reproduction and has virtually no design limitations. In addition consistent ink application allows very long runs, for example 1 000 000 metres/yards plus.

The Flexotex 1900 – 1·8 m (74 in.) wide common impression flexographic printing press, as supplied to James Broadley, Blackburn

In gravure printing the design is engraved into a smooth deposit of copper on the surface of a steel cylinder. A separate cylinder is then engraved for each colour of the design. Each roller revolves in the machine in contact with a pressure cylinder above the engraved roller and ink is supplied to the engraved roller from a colour tray.

Flexographic printing (maximum width (2·6 m/105 in.), max. colours 6)
This process has made some recent advances in quality of the finished print, but the design reproduction costs have also increased thus making very little difference in paper costs to gravure.

This is a roller printing method using an image in relief form usually made from rubber or composit mouldings. As an alternative the printing roller surface may be fully covered with a rubber coating and the design engraved directly into the rubber by a cutting technique. This type of roller is usually used for solid and continuous background colours.

Rotary screen (maximum width 3·3 m–5 m (130 in.–200 in.), maximum colours 6)
The other method of printing which has every indication of becoming the alternative to flexographic printing. Whilst this technique has some design limitations compared with gravure in terms of tonal work, it could cater for a large percentage of the market in terms of price and quality and is ideally suited for small orders (1000–3000 m/yd).

In this process the printing rollers are produced on circular metal screens (40–120 perforations per cm).

Different types of paper printing methods and the resulting relative clarity of line achieved

Near right Rotary screen printed fine line paper. Lines are about 25 thousands of an inch wide to help clarity of line when printing in this method

Centre Fine line definition achieved on a flexographic printing machine. In this illustration the lines are 7–8 thousands of an inch wide

Far right Enlarged photograph of rotary screen printed transfer paper showing certain limitations in terms of line definition, as compared with flexographic printing and gravure printing

Lithographic printing

This traditional paper printing method has also been developed for transfer printing, especially for fine art reproduction work and fine linear designs. This is obviously a single sheet fed process and therefore not suitable for continuous process designs. However this technique is ideally suited for fully fashioned garments, cut and sew panels and motif printing.

This process is an oleophinic technique using an oil type ink, which is applied to a greasy image on a flat or curved plate surrounded by a non-ink reception area usually a wet surface produced on a special plate made from zinc or aluminium. Production from this process can be in excess of 8000 sheets per hour.

Letterpress

This is a similar process to lithographic printing, as it is a non-continuous technique. The design being created by using a raised image on a metal or plastic plate. There are also similarities to the flexographic process, the difference being that a flat plate is used instead of a circular cylinder.

Flat screen

Like lithographic and letterpress this process produces individual sheet transfers. This technique has the unique quality of allowing a very heavy quantity of colour to be printed onto the paper, which is sometimes required in the printing of carpet tiles and other floor coverings; where a heavy laydown is required to penetrate the fabric pile.

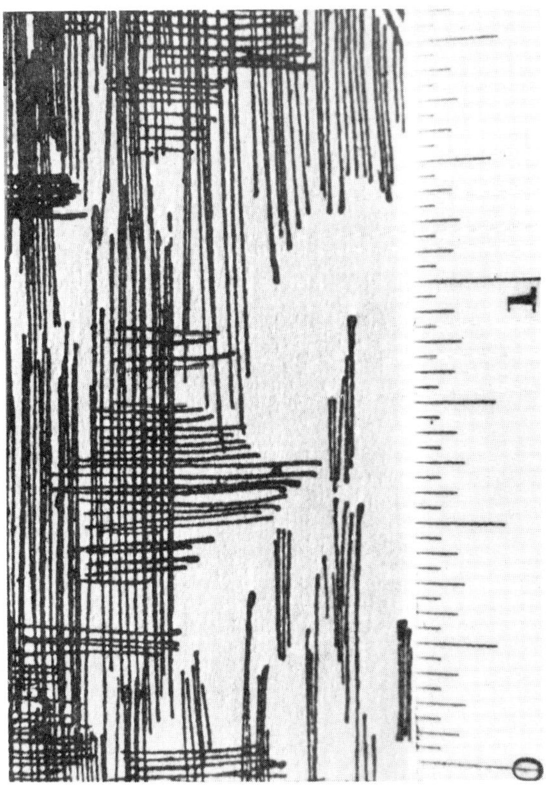

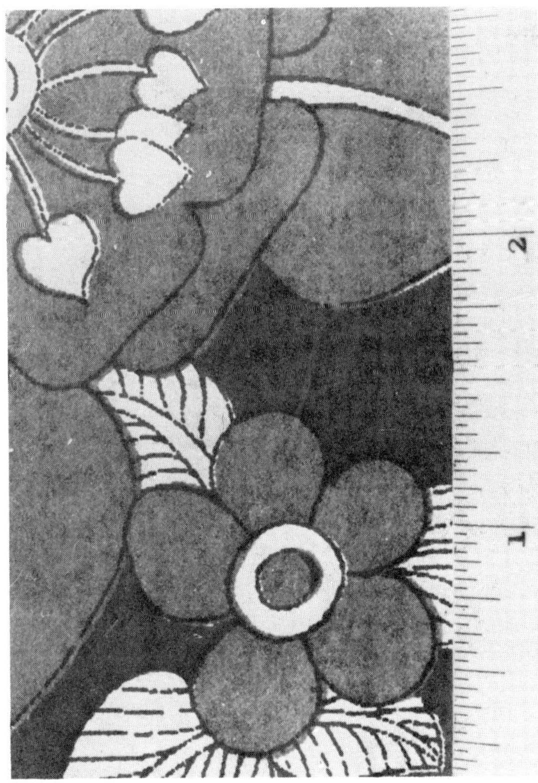

An art-nouveau design printed by lithography. The sophisticated line achieved is typical of this technique. Design by TPI Ltd

Single motif design printed by lithography. Design by TPI Ltd

Litho Printed Designs by TPI Ltd
The process of offset litho printing in terms of transfer printing is becoming increasingle viable, as the relatively inexpensive origination costs allow small unit quantities to be printed at a low cost. This process can be used for a great variety of end products from high fashion and all areas of the garment industry, to more utilitarian items such as bar mats, lamp shades, embroidery patterns, outlines for rug making kits and even souvenir motifs for kitchen items. This process is equally successful in either line or colour

Motif design printed by lithography

Motif design printed by lithography

Detailed single colour design, printed by lithography

A litho printed Zodiac design used as an applied decoration on place mats. The surface of the mat is treated with polyurethane before transfer

A commercial transfer print, which exploits the process to the full. The original transfer paper was gravure printed and the three examples at the top of this sample show different colour-ways

9 Commercial transfer printing machinery

Transfer machines are produced in two different types:
1 The flat bed press which is mainly used for garment printing.
2 The continuous machines which are used for high production runs.

The flat bed presses are available in a variety of types ranging from the single sided units, which are most suitable for schools and colleges, to more sophisticated models which incorporate conveyor or rotary feed systems. Presses are also available which print both sides of a garment simultaneously and one of the latest machines prints first one side and then the other on a conveyor system.

Commercial presses are usually heated by hot oil, electricity or a combination of steam with an electric booster. The production rate from these machines would be from 60–120 printed fully fashioned garments per hour.

A recent innovation in this field is a vacuum press for printing carpet tiles. This machine prints in a vacuum which has the effect of lowering the sublimation temperature of the dyestuffs and so gives high penetration into the carpet pile.

Continuous transfer printing machines are available in several forms, the most common being the type where the paper and fabric pass face to face round a heated cylinder whilst contact is maintained by an endless blanket. These machines are capable of rates up to 1300 yd per hour with designs up to 2 m–2·2 m (80 in.–90 in.) wide.

The second type of continuous calendar is the shoe type and these machines either draw the paper and fabric through a heated metal shoe, similar to a rotary ironing machine, or reverse the process so that the cylinder is heated and a fixed Teflon shoe is brought into contact with the cylinder. The production rate for these machines is lower than the blanket type – approximately 200m/yd per hour, but much wider fabrics can be printed on these machines (3·6 m/12 ft wide).

The most recent machines available use a high suction cylinder to hold the fabric and paper in place and heating is effected by infra-red heaters fitted in a special reflecting chamber. Although production rates are relatively low (approximately 200 m/yd per hour) this process has the great advantage of considerably improving the fabric handle and surface appearance on the finished fabric.

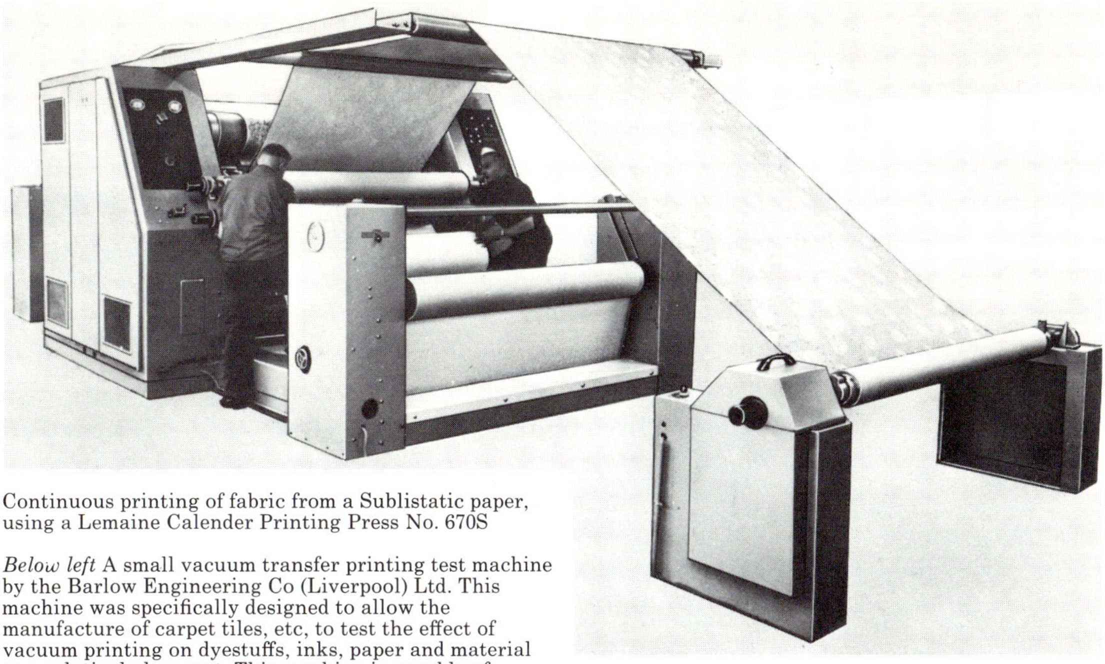

Continuous printing of fabric from a Sublistatic paper, using a Lemaine Calender Printing Press No. 670S

Below left A small vacuum transfer printing test machine by the Barlow Engineering Co (Liverpool) Ltd. This machine was specifically designed to allow the manufacture of carpet tiles, etc, to test the effect of vacuum printing on dyestuffs, inks, paper and material at a relatively low cost. This machine is capable of producing samples up to 15 cm × 15 cm (6 in. × 6 in.) at a temperature of 300°C and at 29 in hg vacuum (operated by a conventional 13 amp plug socket)

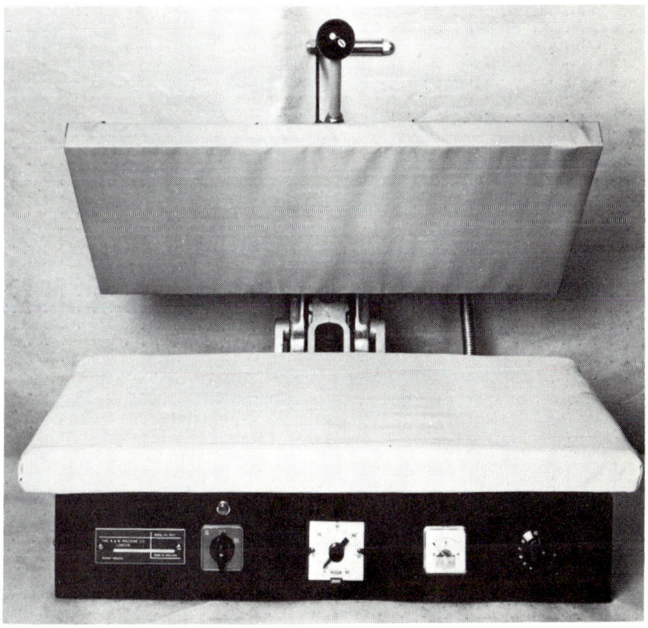

The Taurus 11 flat bed transfer press by B and W Machine Co Ltd, London. This type of press, which has a 66 cm × 35 cm (26 in. × 14 in.) printing bed is ideal for small scale commercial printing, but not suitable for education as the open design creates an obvious safety risk

Colour plate facing
Clowns See pages 54 and 55

Colour plate overleaf
Circles Design by Frank Birtwhistle, photograph by Christopher Hawkins

Transfer printing machines which are appropriate for school use

The relative success of finally transferring the design onto the chosen fabric is very much dependant upon the type of equipment used. This in no way excludes the use of a domestic iron, since excellent results can be achieved using this simple type of heat transfer method. Obviously the choice of iron is important and one should avoid the use of a steam iron if possible as the holes in the base plate can often reoccur on the fabric unless one constantly keeps the iron in motion.

The best type of iron to use is a relatively cheap flat base iron with a good thermostate and a clear warming light. The iron should be regarded as a source of heat rather than a smoothing iron for removing creases. On most fabrics there should be a dwell time of around 20–30 seconds on each area of the design. There is no point in giving exact temperature settings for each fabric as these will vary from different manufacturers and with the age of the iron.

The simplest technique is to test your chosen fabric and design by gradually increasing the temperature from just below 'Cotton' heat on the iron dial, until the heat is just short of melting or discolouring a sample of the fabric. To achieve these results, simply place the fabric in a paper sandwich so that if it melts there is not a molten mass over the sole plate. The controllable variations that can be used at this stage are temperature, time and hardness of the ironing bed. The removal of a felt underlay or paper pad and the substitution of a board can result in a dramatic improvement in terms of transfer, either by using the iron or on the purpose-built small transfer presses.

The various transfer presses illustrated in this chapter are in effect small scale industrial machines. Consequently their temperature control is very accurate and if a dwell warning system is also included it is difficult to achieve a poor result.

The following processing times are applicable for this type of machine:

Polyester, Polyamide, Tricel – 20 seconds at 200°C
Acrylics and Dicel – 15 seconds at 190°C

The use of these sophisticated presses of the front loading type allow more experimental work to be carried out and as we will see in the following chapters many different materials, in addition to fabric, can be printed with this heat transfer technique.

The Labap press was designed for use as a proof printer for transfer printing. The hinged top plate has a heated element and the bottom plate is rigidly mounted in the base of the press. The dimensions of both plates are 28cm × 28cm × 1 cm ($11\frac{1}{4}$ in. × $11\frac{1}{4}$ in. × $\frac{1}{2}$ in.) and the temperature range 130°C to 230°C, 200/240 volts ac 1000 watts

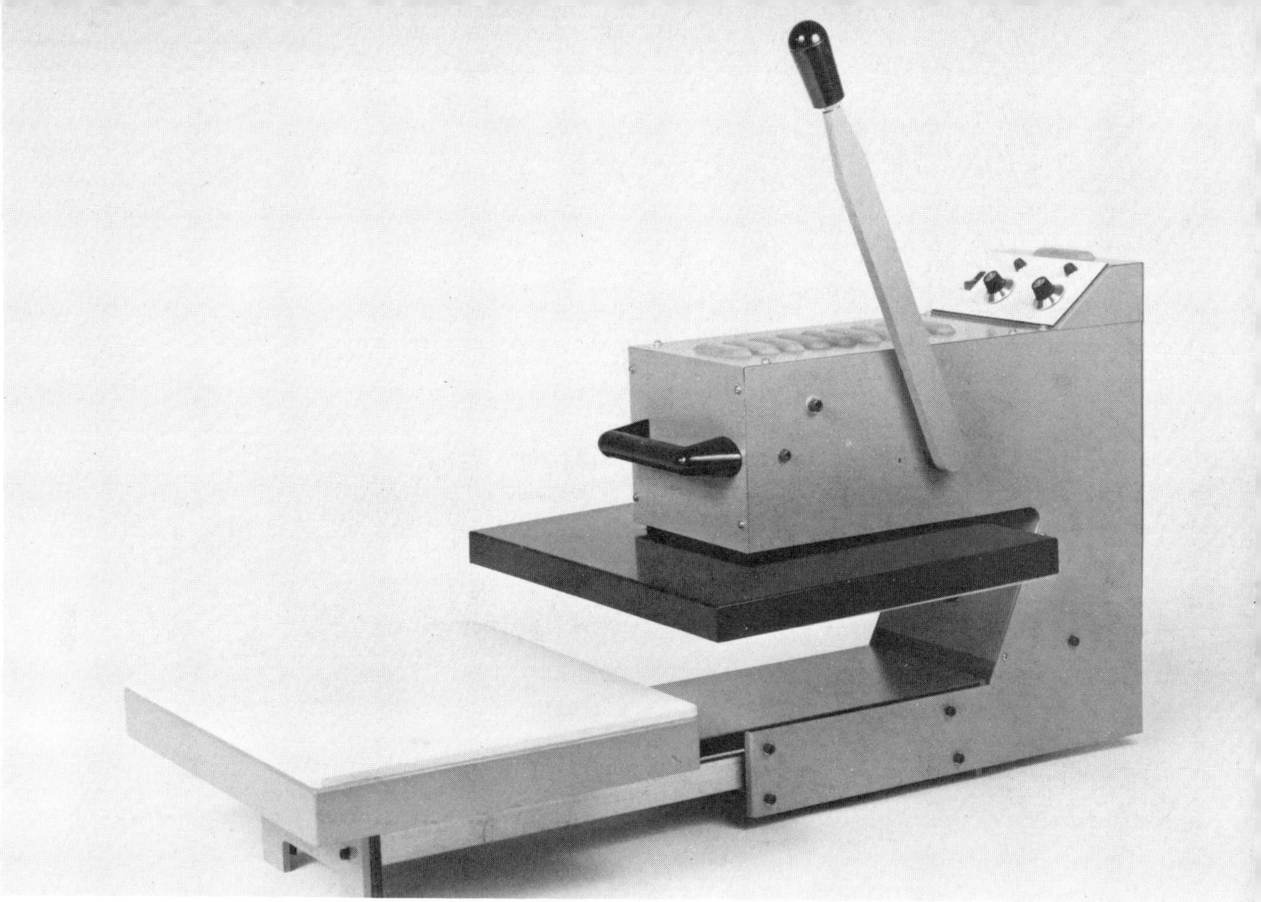

The Double A Manual heat transfer press, manufactured by A Adkins and Sons Ltd, Leicester, suppliers Phipps Faire, Northampton. This relatively small transfer press was designed specifically for the individual designer and education use and consequently has many built-in safety features, such as protective guards and isolation shields. This machine is portable, but generally one would bolt the base plate to a working bench and so create a completely rigid working unit. The specifications are as follows: height 35 cm (14 in.), width 45 cm (18 in.), depth 40 cm (16 in.), transfer area 407 mm × 254 mm (16 in. × 10 in.), heating element 1200 watts, 200/250 volts, temperature controller range 140°C–300°C, electronic audial timer range 0·60 seconds

Small transfer press developed by TPI Ltd, Birmingham includes the following features: plate size 35 cm × 30 cm (14 in. × 12 in.), or 60 cm × 30 cm (24 in. × 12 in.), timer and temperature gauges, fully spring bottom plate to compensate for varying thicknesses of fabric, temperature range 0°C to 300°C, positive action head lowering lever, total weight 28·5 kilos

The Ibis HT52 installed at Leicester Polytechnic Department of Printed Textiles. This industrial press is manufactured by Ibis Engineering of Kendle, Cumberland and has a printing bed measuring 1·8 m × 0·9 m (6 ft × 3 ft). The base is steam heated and the top electrically heated. The printing operation is operated by compressed air. Heat control and dwell time are electronically controlled

Above Preparing the press for printing

Setting the press in motion

After printing the fabric the press head is raised automatically to reveal the completed design

Checking the finished print for registration and colour intensity

The Double A Manual transfer press in operation at an In-Service workshop on transfer printing

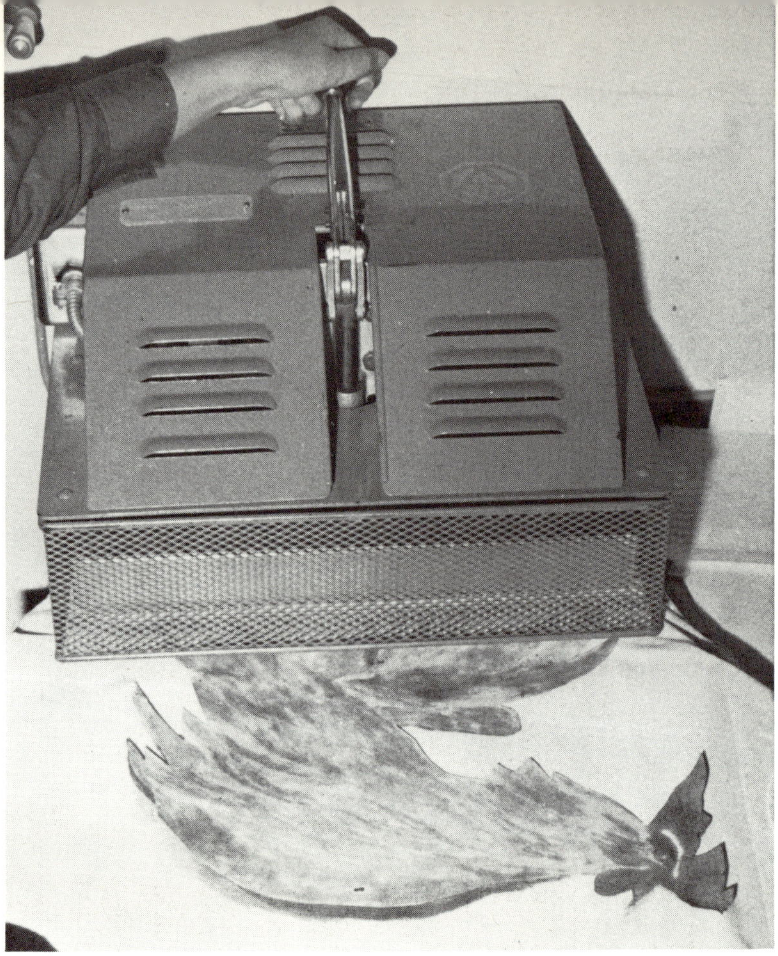

The sliding table fitted to the model which allows accurate work location and yet complete safety when the press is in operation

10 The transfer printing of materials other than synthetic fabrics

Natural fibres

Ideally the heat transfer method of printing designs should be successful on all surfaces, but, as we have already seen disperse dyes have no substantivity for natural fibres and consequently do not produce commercially acceptable results. There has, however, been a great amount of research into this area and already a number of companies have produced ways of printing which allow natural materials, such as wool and leather to be printed in a technique which is closely related to conventional transfer printing. Interesting work is also being carried out into ways of treating natural fibres with a synthetic medium so that the transfer colours can be applied permanently to the surface, whether it be cotton or hessian. This development is of obvious interest to the art teacher as it would greatly increase the scope of the print process.

Below is a brief summary of some of the methods which have been developed to print materials other than synthetic fabrics by transfer printing techniques.

Wool

The two main ways of working in this technique are *batch* processing and *continuous* processing and most of the commercial work to date uses method one, which is carried out onto knitted (fully fashioned) or cut and sew seamed up garments.

As can be seen from the illustrations, body shapes with separate collars and trimmings are produced which are then immersed in a viscose paste and put through a squeezing mangle to give a paste to fibre pick up of 250%.

The framed shapes which are cut out of a laminated plastic called Pirtoid are then placed inside the body shape so that the garment is stretched approximately 12%. This extension being necessary to enable the colour to penetrate down into the seams of the garment. The framed garment is then laid onto the transfer paper which has been printed in 100 m/yd lengths using dyes that have been specially selected.

The next stage sees a sandwich of printed paper, framed garment and a second sheet of printed paper, laid on a Hoffman type press which gives a squeezed pressure of approximately 20·6 KN/m^2 (3 lb per sq in.). Live or closed steam heating then transfers the colour in a period varying from 4 to 6 minutes. After this the garments are removed from the frame, they are batched up and sent forward to conventional scouring and milling.

For the most efficient usage of paper the collars and trimmings are printed separately and to give the necessary extension of the fabric the collars, etc, are stretched across Velcro tape.

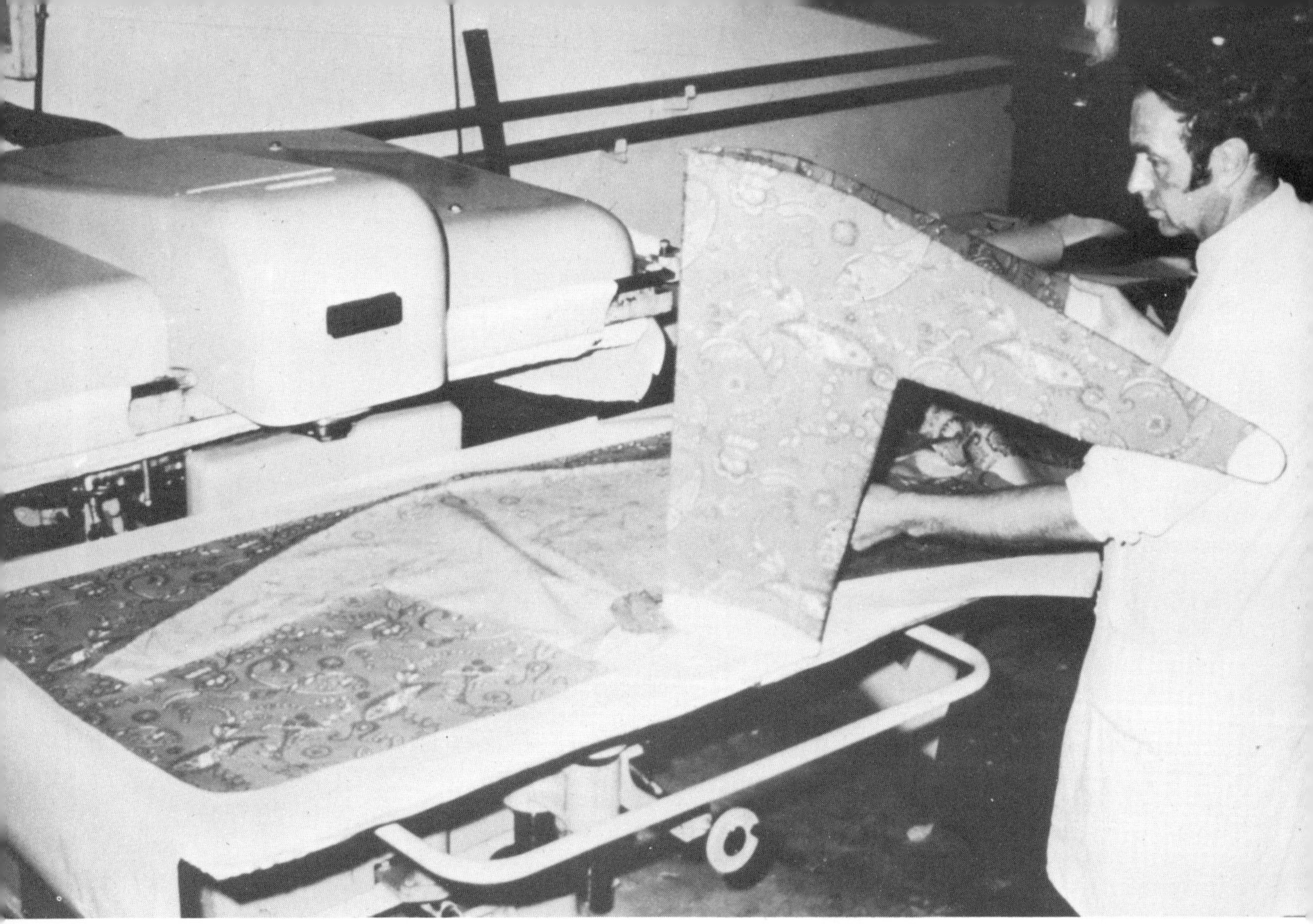

Equipment required for transfer

In recent years there has been a considerable development from the simple Hofmann presses to custom built machines where the heat required is provided by the use of radio frequency energy. These machines give an extreme uniformity of temperature control and therefore give a high degree of dye fastness onto the cashmere, wool, carpet tiles, etc, which are being printed.

Other developments in this field show the completion of the continuous printing machine which will accept any fabric woven or knitted, made from any fibre or fibre blend, and these machines have the capacity of printing through the wet route, as well as through the dry sublimable route. One also sees the possibility of using this type of machine incorporating radio frequency heating methods to print broad loom carpets and therefore greatly reduce the pollution factor in this area of textile production.

Leather

A large volume of suitably prepared hides are now being printed by heat transfer techniques. In this method the leather is given an acrylic or melamine type finish and the skin pre-shrunk at a temperature slightly in excess of the actual transfer print temperature, ie pre-shrunk at 205°C for 30 seconds and transferred at 200°C for 30 seconds.

More recently the Shoe and Allied Trades Research Association, in conjunction with a leading transfer paper manufacturer, has produced a new technique for printing polyurethane shoe uppers. In this method the specially prepared paper is positioned face to face with the upper material and heat transferred for approximately 30 seconds. The 'spent' paper and the printed material are then separated and a simple spray shoeroom finishing treatment applied. At the moment this *Satraprint* process is used only onto PU coated fabrics, but research is also being carried out onto other materials for the shoe industry.

Wood and hardboard laminates

These can also be printed to a commercial standard providing they have been first pre-treated with a suitable paint or varnish such as those based on polyester, melamine and acrylic. This coating has to be pre-cured otherwise sticking of the paper to the print surface will occur. Transfer printing conditions are similar to textiles, ie 200°C at 30 seconds.

Aluminium

Anodised aluminium can also be heat transfer printed, as shown on page 131 (top) but great care has to be given to ink selection and surface preparation. Firms are already selling transfer inks and decorated papers which will successfully print on this material and the potential is obviously enormous in terms of decorating such items as kitchen ware.

Other materials which can be printed

Also in this area of research one sees the potential of printing Melinex which is a polyester film coated with aluminium deposited on one side. This side can be identified by scratching each side with a pin and holding it up to the light. The reverse side to the aluminium can be transferred at 200°C for 20 seconds. This gives some very interesting results which may be further enhanced by selectively removing certain areas of the

Opposite Wool transfer process. The garment is immersed in a viscous paste and stretched over a pre-cut frame made from laminated plastic

The above illustrates the Hofmann type press being prepared for printing. The first printed paper is laid down onto the bed. The framed garment is then layed onto the paper and a second paper placed in position.

After transfer the printed garment is taken from the press and the body frame carefully removed. Each transfer takes from 4 to 6 minutes. The garment then has to be batched up and sent forward to conventional scouring and milling processes

aluminium with a weak solution of caustic soda. This gives a mirror side with coloured areas etched out as transparent inserts.

Perspex sheet may be printed at 160°C for 2 to 3 minutes as well as Styrene which can be treated in the same way as Perspex. Obviously it is essential to carry out small trials first, as one is approaching the melting point of these plastics. This also makes it necessary to take the plastic sheet off the press whilst hot and sandwich it between weighted boards whilst it cools down to minimise distortion. The transfer paper may also stick to the surface but this can be removed by soaking in warm water. This area of work is I feel particularly interesting in terms of vacuum forming, as the sheet used can be printed in this technique before forming and so create unusual distortions.

Cotton

Finally we look at the possibility of printing cotton by heat transfer printing and as one would expect many of the avenues already discussed for other materials have been tested in terms of cotton fabrics, with varying degrees of success and a number of patents have been taken out. However, the answer to this problem is not only one of satisfactory transfer, which one imagines will be successfully overcome in the near future. But also one of economics, for obviously the resulting process must be competitive with the traditional methods of printing this fabric.

Finally one sees that any successful method of printing cotton must be equal in terms of fabric handle to the conventional methods and above all the colour fastness must be acceptable to the existing commercial standards. In terms of textile printing projects in schools, I can see how the traditional methods of decoration such as tie dye and batik would emphasise cotton fabrics, whereas the new technology developed through transfer printing could give the students an opportunity to work with a wide range of synthetic fibres and allied surfaces.

Below and opposite A series of transferred designs printed on wool, using the printing route described in the series of process shots on page 126

The three illustrations show the prize winning shoes in a competition organized to give young designers the opportunity to exploit the wide potential of the heat transfer printing process in show design. The designs show a variety of textures which have been transfer printed onto the specially finished PU coated upper material manufactured by Brymor Ltd. The transfer papers have been specially developed by Alf Coope Ltd of Leeds and this has been a joint venture with The Shoe and Allied Trades Research Association of Kettering

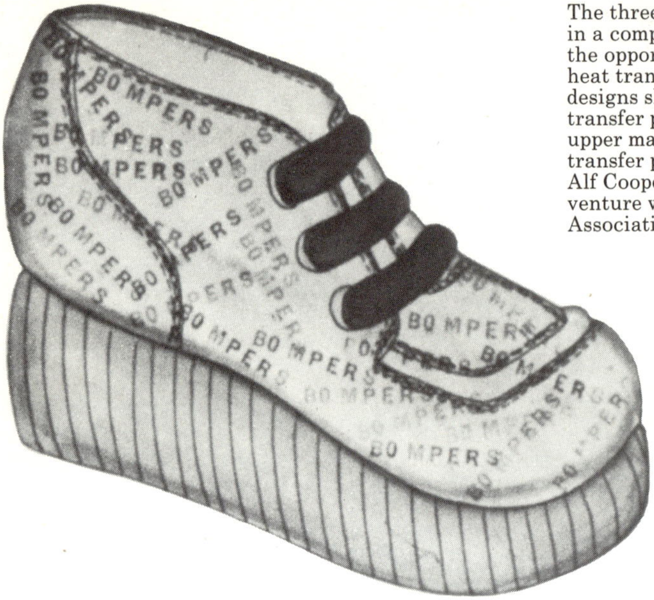

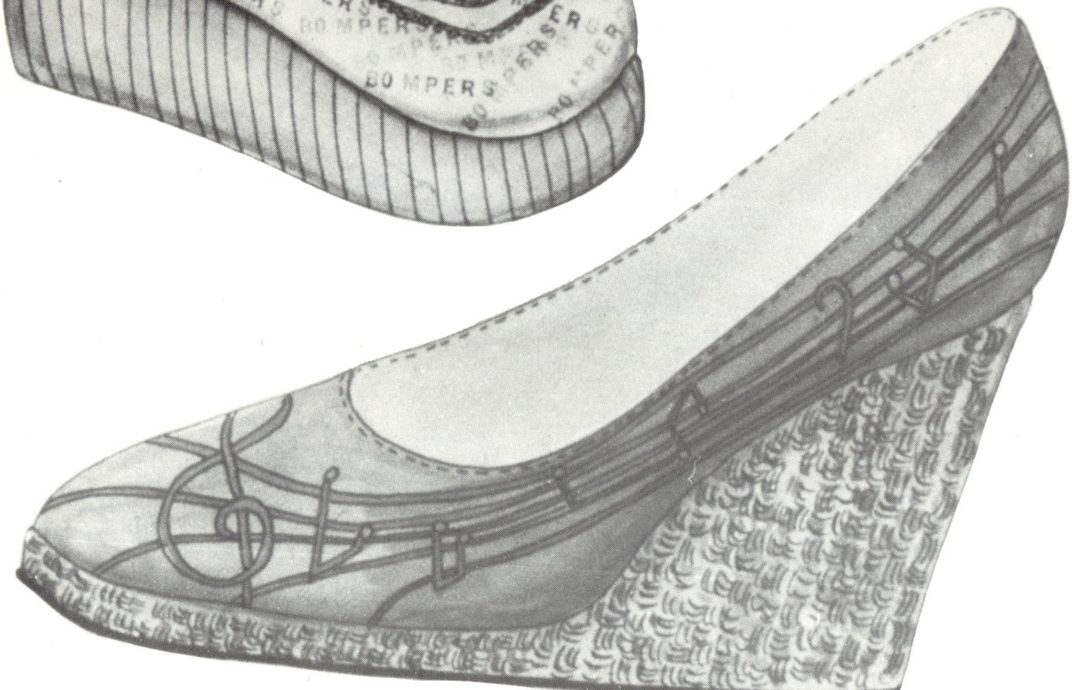

Base material by Ano-coil Ltd, showing the potential of heat transfer printing pre-anodised aluminium. The panels on the extreme right show printed aluminium wall tiles. The back panel is a suspended ceiling section, in simulated wood grain. The large coiled samples illustrate the variety of surfaces available in this process. The squared section on the left is a decorated face for an automatic control box. The three tube sections illustrate the potential of decorating this material, for such items as garden furniture. Finally the collection of small items illustrates the variety of household products made from aluminium which could be enriched in this heat transfer technique

A melamine place mat which has been transfer printed in a brightly coloured design. The resulting design is not only heat resistant and permanent but is also completely abrasive resistant as the design has become a part of the melamine surface. Ceramics by Ray Finch

In this example a heat transfer design has been transferred to anodized aluminium. Intense colours and very high quality printed designs, including four-colour half-tone printing, can be produced on suitably anodized aluminium. In this technique the colour penetrates the anodized layer and therefore is not a surface print; consequently a high abrasion resistance is obtained. Design produced in Marler Tex inks

11 Research and possible developments

As I have been aware when preparing this book the theoretical aspects of transfer printing are being widely studied by different organisations around the world, and many interesting papers and articles are being published almost every month, in such trade magazines as the British Knitting Industry. If advanced students wish to carry on their own studies the 1974 July issue of *The Journal of the Society of Dyers and Colourists* reporting the work of Dr Jones of Leeds would be of relevance.* For here he deals with some of the basic aspects of transfer printing, in terms of investigating a number of parameters involved in the heat transfer print process. In addition I have listed my own sources of reference so these can be studied in more detail, as obviously one can only summarise many of the print processes under discussion.

There is no doubt that many more papers and indeed books, will be written on all aspects of transfer printing in the future, but there is no substitute for personal and practical research and here the student, with the minimum of equipment, could make a very worthwhile contribution to this relatively new textile process.

What of the future developments? Already one sees the very real potential of creating environments where every item in the room, from furnishings, carpets, wall coverings and moulded furniture could all be transfer printed with the same design and colour combinations.

At another level one sees the introduction of space-age technology in the use of laser-beam engravings for gravure printing and colleges using computers to create designs for transfer printing. In this area of development I recently saw demonstrated a vacuum operated screen printing machine which had been adapted for the production of transfer papers, and so creating an ideal method of printing multiple design motifs for transfer printing.

Finally one must return to the educational potential of this process and although this technique can be criticised as it does not work on some fabrics, I feel a more positive approach should be adopted and the students encouraged to explore all the different surfaces which can be successfully transfer printed. This technique was developed specifically to work onto man-made fabrics and therefore makes a real contribution to the world as we know it today.

*Dr C E Vellins, *British Knitting Industries Journal.*

Transfer printing is not confined to apparel; here is a transfer printed table cloth. Design by Sublistatic

Two commercial prints created from photographic originals. The papers were printed by lithography and then transferred onto polyester. This type of design work is mainly used in the 'trendy' pop market and to decorate souvenir items

A wide selection of transfer printed items from The Studio of Binney and Smith, New York (makers of Crayola crayons). All pieces are by Holly Diane Shaw, except where specified. (1) Butterfly kite, with silver sequins and silver tail. (2) Stuffed quilted stitchery piece. (3) Pinafore, completed over a grid rubbing (4) Three stuffed dolls and one dinosaur (a) Tulsilla ballerina, rubbings and tulle sequins and woolhair (b) Isabelle with fan, ribbon with fabric crayon hearts, sequins (c) Felix the Strong Man, fabric crayon (d) Dinosaur, rubbings with felt scales, button eyes. (5) Animal jingle pillow by Carol Durham. (6) Squeezable foam blocks covered with fabric crayon designs and embroidered eyes. (7) Table napkin. (8) Quilt

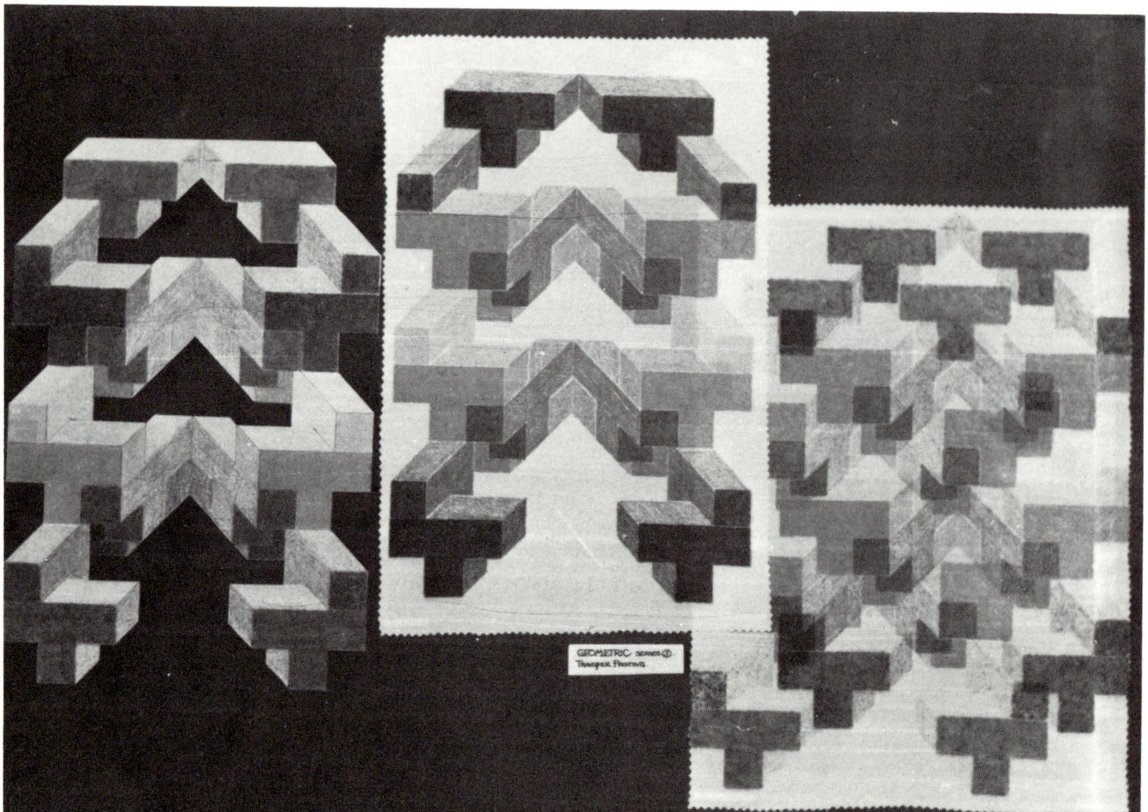

A sophisticated design series by Peter Barker. On the left the geometric paper original which has been coloured with transfer crayons and then cut out accurately. The middle panel shows the reverse design printed onto cimplene and the right hand design shows the effect achieved when the original paper is printed a second and third time

Manufacturers and sources of reference

The author wishes to thank the following for their assistance in the preparation of this book.

A Luff, Adkins and Sons Ltd, Leicester
B Turner, Ano-Coil Ltd, Milton Keynes, Bucks
J Weisfield, B and W Transprint Ltd, London
L Mills, Barlow Engineering Co (Liverpool) Ltd, Liverpool
N J P Tansley, Bemrose Corporation, Derby
G Lampros, Binney and Smith, New York
P J Day, Binney and Smith (Europe) Ltd, Bedford
Eugene P Dempsey, Editor, British Knitting Industry
J A Rose, Coates Bros, London
G A Smith, Dawson International Ltd, Selkirk, Scotland
E Driver, Fishburn Inks, Watford
Mrs F A Keir, ICI Fibres, London
Dr C E Vellins, L B Holliday Ltd, Huddersfield
S Woodward, Labap Transfer Presses, Huddersfield
M Hubinet, Lefranc et Bourgeois, Le Mans, France
J W Bird, E T Marler Ltd, Wimbledon, London
G Clarke, Monsanto, Leicester
J W Pardoe, Phipps Faire, Northampton
P D A Lacey, Shoe and Allied Trades Research Association, Kettering
T B Cotton, Sketchley Dyers and Finishers, Hinckley
M Ehrwein, Sublistatic SA, Geneva
E J White, Sublistatic Ltd, Leicester
Miss J Bodin, Strachan and Henshaw, Bristol
J Davidson, Transfer Process Innovators Ltd, Birmingham
J S O'Neill, Transprint (UK) Ltd, Manchester

In addition to the persons listed above, the author would also like to acknowledge the following reference material which has been used in the preparation of this book.

A Review of the Literature Relating to Heat Transfer Printing, a Review Paper by Nicholas L Moore, Lecturer Watford College of Technology

Technical Information on Heat Transfer Printing of Acrylic Fabrics issued by Monsanto Ltd

Paper Printing as related to Heat Transfer Printing, a Technical Paper by G Arnold Winterburn, American IWER Corp, Greenville SC

British Knitting Industry Journal

Vol 46 – No 527	Transfer Printing Index (A–Z Directory)
Vol 47 – No 540	Transfer Printing Index: Guide to Supplies and Services; Transfer Printing; The Role of the Man-made Fibre Product
Vol 47 – No 542	International Transfer Printing Seminar
Vol 47 – No 543	Rotary Screen Equipment for Transfer Printing
Vol 47 – No 546	The Impact of Transfer Printing on the Conventional Printer; also a Review of Recent Developments
Vol 47 – No 547	Transfer Printing Terylene and Crimplene
Vol 48 – No 548	Transfer Printing Men's Wear

Knitting World

May 1975	Widening the Frontiers in Transfer Paper Printing
June 1975	Transfer Printing Index 75

Identification of Textile Materials (7th edition) edited by Carolyn A Farnfield and D R Perry, The Textile Institute, 10 Blackfriars Street, Manchester M3 5DR. This book contains detailed analytical methods of textile fibre identification and the analysis of fibre blends.

Recommended reading

A series of lectures on transfer printing co-edited by Dr Vellins and Eugene Dempsey entitled *Heat Transfer Printing*, published by Interprint, 10–12 Yardley Wood Road, Birmingham 14

Suppliers

Transfer crayons
Manufactured under the trade name of Finart Fabricrayons by Binney and Smith (Europe) Ltd, Ampthill Road, Bedford.

Available from:

Thomas Hope and Sankey Ltd
Royton Rug Mill
St Phillips Drive, Royton
near Oldham, Lancashire

B Garrod Ltd
Waters Lane, Kings Langley
Hertfordshire

Alpen Ltd
2 Westway Gardens
Croydon, Surrey

Craftsmith
PO Box 1
Greenbridge Industrial Estate
Swindon, Wiltshire

John Menzies Ltd
59/61 High Street
Montrose, Angus
Scotland

Nottingham Handcraft Co
Melton Road, West Bridgford
Nottingham NG2 6HD

L A Parnham
24–36 Queens Road
Nottingham

David Williams
25 Bridge Street Row
Chester

John Menzies Ltd
50 Old Brompton Road
London SW7

Dunn Art Stores
35 Scott Street
Perth PH1 5EH

Transfer inks (aqueous)

Ploton Sundries Ltd
273 Archway Road
London N6
Suppliers of transfer colours in 30 cc jars, 12 colours, mail order service available.

Keegan Brico Tetley Chemicals Ltd
55–57 Glengall Road
London SE15 6NQ
Suppliers of transfer colours in concentrated form under the trade name Dispersol Colours, available in minimum 1 kg lots, further details and price list available on request.

L B Holliday and Co Ltd
Leeds Road, Huddersfield
Suppliers of transfer printing pastes suitable for screen printing, sold under the trade name Sublaprint 70600 Range. A full colour range is available, and also an extending agent known as S P Paste. Minimum order of 1 kilo. Information and price list available on request.

Algenate

Algenate Industries
22 Henrietta Street
London WC2
Algenate is also available from some art shops and large chemists.

Transfer inks (spirit based)

E T Marler Ltd
Deer Park Road
Wimbledon
London SW19 3UE
Suppliers of Marler Tex sublistic screen inks. Extender and thinning agent also supplied, minimum order 1 kilo, information and price list available on request.

Coates Bros Inks Ltd
Cray Avenue, St Mary Cray
Orpington, Kent
Suppliers of Alkatex Screen Inks in 16 different colours. Minimum order 5 kilos. Technical information and price list available on request.

Fishburn Printing Ink Co
94 St Albans Road
Watford WD2 4BU
Suppliers of Screentran Colours and Medium, available in quarter, half, and 1 kilo containers. Lithotran inks for litho printing transfer papers are also available in the same size containers. Educational discounts are given and technical information and price list are available on request.

Vilene

Vilene Ltd
PO Box 3, Greetland
Halifax, W Yorkshire
Information on the use of *Vilene* also price list and samples on request.

Job lots of synthetic fabrics, ideal for experimental work, available from a number of firms who advertise in the weekly magazine *Exchange and Mart*.

Suppliers in the USA

Transfer crayons

Beckley Cardy Co
Hayward, California 94545

Stationers Corp
Los Angeles, California 90055

Zellerbach Paper Co
So. San Francisco
California 94080

Beckley Cardy Co
Chicago, Illinois 60639

J L Hammett Co
Braintree, Massachusetts 02184
Zellerbach Paper Co
Seattle, WA 98124

J L Hammett Co
Union, New Jersey 07083

Baker and Taylor
Central Islip, NY 11722

Arthur Brown and Bros
New York, NY 10017

Kurtz Bros
Paoli, Pennsylvania 19301

Practical Drawing Co
Dallas, Texas 75215

American Crayon Co
1706 Hayes Ave., Sandusky
0.44870

Chemical Manufacturing Co
444 Madison Ave.
New York, N.Y. 10010

J.L. Hammett Co
100 Hammett Pl. Braintree
Ma. 02184

I C I Organics, Inc
55 Canal St. Providence
R.I. 02903

PRO Chemical & Dye Co
Box 1192 Fairfield
Ct. 06430

Sax Arts & Crafts
Box 2002 Milwaukee
Wis. 53201

Triarco Arts & Crafts
110–112 W. Carpenter Ave, Wheeling
Ill. 60090

Spirit-based transfer inks and supporting media

Colonial Printing Ink Co
180 East Union Avenue
East Rutherford
New Jersey 07073

Inmont Corporation
1133 Avenue of the Americas
New York, NY 10036

Index